A garden project workbook

fences *and* hedges

A garden project workbook

fences *and* hedges

and other garden dividers

Richard Bird

photography by **Stephen Robson**

STEWART, TABORI & CHANG
NEW YORK

First published in 1998 under the title
Creating Boundaries and Screens by

Ryland Peters & Small
Cavendish House
51-55 Mortimer Street
London W1N 7TD

Published in 1999 and distributed in the U.S.
by Stewart, Tabori & Chang,
a division of U.S. Media Holdings, Inc.
115 West 18th Street, New York, NY 10011

Distributed in Canada by
General Publishing Company Ltd.
30 Lesmill Road
Don Mills, Ontario, Canada, M3B 2T6

Library of Congress Cataloging-in-Publication Data

Bird, Richard.
    Fences and hedges and other garden
dividers/by Richard Bird; photography by Stephen
Robson.
            p. cm. — (Garden project workbooks)
    Includes index
    ISBN 1-55670-836-X
    1. Hedges. 2. Fences. 3. Screens (Plants). 4.
Walls I. Title. II. Series.
SB437.B48 1999
635.9—dc21   98-17156
                                    CIP

Printed in China
10 9 8 7 6 5 4 3 2 1

Designers **Liz Brown, Vicky Holmes,
                    Mark Latter**

Editors **Sarah Polden, Ann Snyder**

Production **Meryl Silbert**

contents

All gardens have to have boundaries, something to limit them and to prevent them from merging with the neighboring yard. In the past, boundaries were purely protective, to keep animals and undesirable visitors out. Today, they still perform this function, but they also have other purposes, including preserving privacy and reducing the interference of outside noise.

Within the garden, boundaries can be used to divide or screen the space or to delineate different areas. Screens can hide trash cans or they can create a sense of mystery, guarding part of the garden from the viewer who feels compelled to investigate; similarly, an archway can mark two different areas of the garden, allowing only a glimpse of one from the other, while pathways might join two areas or separate them, creating a boundary between the lawn and a flower bed. Internal boundaries can be permanent, such as a stream, or temporary, such as the summer display of tall, bright annuals.

As well as having a practical function, boundaries are excellent for decorating the garden. They can be decorative in their own right, seen in a beautiful hedge or striking pleached trees, or they can be used to support and protect plants, a wall, fence, or trellis covered by a scrambling climber. Boundaries create a backdrop against which the rest of the garden can be seen, setting the tone for the design and the planting.

In their various ways, boundaries are a very important part of any garden, and in this book we offer practical and imaginative suggestions for making the most of your needs and desires.

above Use the shelter and warmth offered by a wall to grow tender plants such as grapes. They will respond well and are an unusual and appealing sight.

left A traditional, period house can take exuberant growth – but not at the cost of light. Allow climbers to grow around windows but not over or through them!

below A bold plaque, effective tile work, and lush foliage create a well-balanced prospect. Look for garden ornaments that reflect the age and style of your home.

walls are the most solid of garden boundaries and usually mark

the perimeter of the garden, be it the house or garden wall. They very much

set the tone of the whole planting display, offering a versatile canvas for

abundant climbers, restrained architectural displays, mounted containers,

or water spouts and ornaments. A plain wall can be covered with growth,

an attractive one highlighted by foliage and flowers.

above Seasonal interest is a
priority for walls that are so
much on view. The leaves of
this climber are turning for
their autumn show.

right If your garden is large
enough to offer a vista, then
take advantage of it. Here,
the very absence of part of
the wall leads the eye to the
next point of interest.

above Fruit trees bring
homey comfort to a garden
and a trained plant adds
order without formality.

left Roses, rightly a constant
favorite, give a glorious
performance when they
have a large wall to cover.

house wall

ONE OF THE MOST satisfying aspects of gardening is to integrate the house successfully into the overall garden design. The use of climbers and wall shrubs is a very effective way of achieving this. Climbing plants not only help to unify the scheme but they can also transform a house, softening lines and bringing seasonal interest. Fragrant climbers, such as the rose 'Mme Alfred Carrière', grown around windows can fill a room with perfume during the summer.

materials & equipment

30 vine eyes
30 ft (9 m) galvanized wire
1 bucket of well-rotted organic material
1 *Rosa* 'Mme Alfred Carrière' or similar climber
4 canes
plant ties

hammer, pliers, pruners, spade

STAGE 6

pruning, year 2, early spring

The rose will have flowered on the previous year's growth. Cut this old growth back to a main stem to encourage flowering and cut out any unhealthy or weak, leafless growth. Check the ties and secure any new growth throughout the growing season. 'Mme Alfred Carrière' produces clusters of double creamy-white blooms during the summer and into the autumn.

STAGE 7

maintaining established climber, early spring

Encourage a broad, curving shape by pruning old stems by two-thirds of their length. Continue to prune out less productive, diseased, and spindly stems and remove suckers. This climber can grow 18 ft (5.5 m) tall and some 10 ft (3 m) wide.

Care and Maintenance

- *Deadhead throughout the flowering season to encourage new blooms.*
- *Regularly check that the vine eyes and wires are secure. As the climber matures, they will be bearing a growing weight.*

STAGE 1

fixing eyes

Climbing roses need a firm support and wires are ideal. These are held against the wall with vine eyes (right) that are hammered or screwed into place.

wedge shaped   **screw-in eye**   **screw-in hook eye**

STAGE 2

attaching wires

Secure the vine eyes at 24-in (60-cm) intervals in rows 12–18 in (30–45 cm) apart. Feed galvanized wire (which does not rust) through the eyes and twist it around the end eyes to hold it taut.

STAGE 3

planting the rose

Never plant tight against a wall; the soil here is usually very dry, so dig a hole at least 12 in (30 cm) away. This should be larger than the root ball. Add plenty of organic material before planting, spread the roots, and fill the hole. Train the plant to the wall using a cane.

STAGE 4

training the rose

A climber like *Rosa* 'Mme Alfred Carrière' will fan out as it grows. The stems will need to be tied to the wirework support but do not pull or force them.

STAGE 5

pruning and training, year 1, summer

Tie in new stems to establish fanned growth, training shoots out along the wires where possible. Remove any dead, diseased, or damaged growth. Prune the tips of vigorous, straight main shoots to encourage branching. Make an angled cut just above a leaf or bud.

garden wall

GARDEN WALLS come in all shapes and sizes, some beautiful in their own right, others less attractive. Plants can be used in a variety of ways either to enhance the wall's appearance or to conceal it. Walls can be the perfect visual foil for plants, supplying a neutral backdrop for informal and formal displays alike. They also provide physical support and protection. Where space is limited, walls can carry containers filled with seasonal plants or work with an elegantly planted raised bed.

materials & equipment

wall support
3 vine eyes for the first yd (m) then
2 per yd (m)
galvanized wire to cover the length of the
wall plus 12 in (30 cm) for securing,
multiplied by the number of tiers required
drill, hammer, pliers

planting
3 buckets of organic material per sq yd
(sq m)
plants (*see plan opposite*)
3 3-ft (1-m) canes for the wall plants
plant ties

fork, spade, rake, trowel, pruners,
watering can

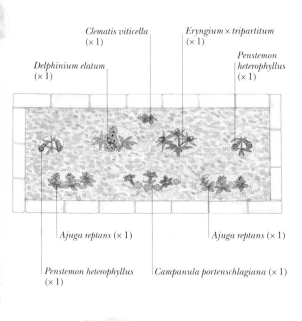

Clematis viticella
(× 1)

Delphinium elatum
(× 1)

Eryngium × tripartitum
(× 1)

Penstemon heterophyllus
(× 1)

Ajuga reptans (× 1)

Ajuga reptans (× 1)

Penstemon heterophyllus
(× 1)

Campanula portenschlagiana (× 1)

a town-garden wall

Raised beds, here 6 × 2 ft (180 × 60 cm), are ideal where space is limited. Couple whitewash with cool blue plants. Avoid such beds on house walls as they can cause damp.

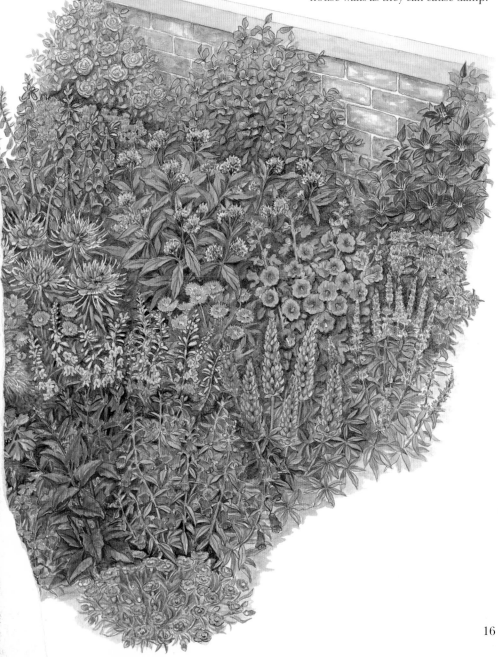

planning a wall-side bed

If you have the opportunity to create a scheme from scratch, take time to plan the design. Consider the character of the existing wall, here a well-aged structure of warm terra-cotta bricks, and complement it with your chosen plants. Select plants that will both benefit from protection and give good height at the rear of the bed. Use shorter plants at the front.

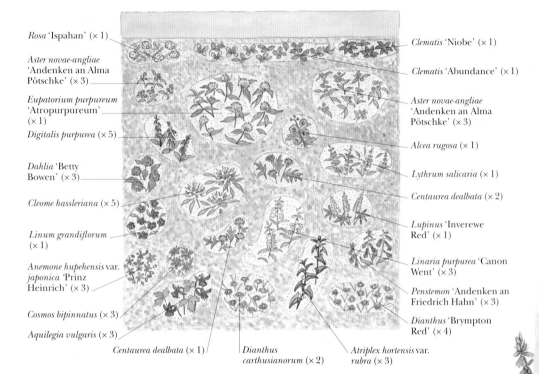

Rosa 'Ispahan' (× 1)

Aster novae-angliae 'Andenken an Alma Pötschke' (× 3)

Eupatorium purpureum 'Atropurpureum' (× 1)

Digitalis purpurea (× 5)

Dahlia 'Betty Bowen' (× 3)

Cleome hassleriana (× 5)

Linum grandiflorum (× 1)

Anemone hupehensis var. *japonica* 'Prinz Heinrich' (× 3)

Cosmos bipinnatus (× 3)

Aquilegia vulgaris (× 3)

Centaurea dealbata (× 1)

Dianthus carthusianorum (× 2)

Atriplex hortensis var. *rubra* (× 3)

Clematis 'Niobe' (× 1)

Clematis 'Abundance' (× 1)

Aster novae-angliae 'Andenken an Alma Pötschke' (× 3)

Alcea rugosa (× 1)

Lythrum salicaria (× 1)

Centaurea dealbata (× 2)

Lupinus 'Inverewe Red' (× 1)

Linaria purpurea 'Canon Went' (× 3)

Penstemon 'Andenken an Friedrich Hahn' (× 3)

Dianthus 'Brympton Red' (× 4)

planting the bed

This bed runs across 6 ft (1.8 m) of the wall and is 10 ft (3 m) long. Check that the wall is in good condition as, once growth has been established, access will be much more difficult. Secure wires to the wall to support the climbers (see page 11). Prepare the ground well in the autumn by removing perennial weeds and digging it thoroughly, adding generous quantities of organic material. In the spring, remove any weeds that have appeared and prepare to plant (in areas with mild winters, the ground can be prepared in the spring and planted in autumn). Position the plants in their pots and plant from the back of the bed to the front. Plant the rose and the clematis at least 12 in (30 cm) away from the wall (see page 11).

Care and Maintenance

- *'Abundance' is a Group 3 clematis that requires hard pruning while 'Niobe' is Group 2 that needs lighter pruning (see page 99).*

- *Prune the rose immediately after flowering, cutting main shoots by a third and side shoots by two-thirds.*

- *On windy sites, support the taller freestanding perennials.*

- *Deadhead throughout the summer.*

fruit wall

WALLS CAN SUSTAIN plants that are both productive and decorative: all manner of fruits can be trained to take on elegant, geometric shapes. Apples and pears can be grown as cordons and, as here, espaliers, while plums, peaches, and nectarines are excellent for fan training. These traditional forms have graced walls for centuries. Figs, grapes, passion fruit, and all manner of currants and berries can also be grown against a wall that will provide warmth and protection to the growing plant.

materials & equipment

9 vine eyes
30 ft (9 m) galvanized wire
1 maiden pear tree
3 canes
plant ties
1 bucket of well-rotted organic material

hammer, pliers, pruners, spade

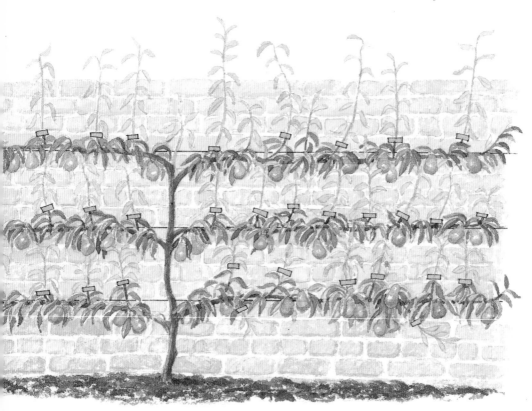

STAGE 5

the established espalier

Once the arms of the topmost tier are well established, prune back the central leader to just above this tier in the summer. The lateral growth can also be cut back if the allotted space has been filled. To maintain the plant, continue to prune shoots on the lateral stems to three leaves above the basal cluster and shorten side shoots to a leaf.

Care and Maintenance

- *Established espaliers will require winter pruning to thin out overcrowded and unproductive spurs (short branches). This should be done as necessary, not annually.*

- *An espalier must be pruned regularly and well if it is to retain its formal symmetry.*
- *The wall will carry a heavy weight so it should be checked for signs of wear.*

protection from frost

When the first buds appear, the tree is most susceptible to frost damage. To protect it at night, create a framework of angled canes that project away from the plant and roll down woven nylon netting to cover the full height and width of the tree. This will create shelter without harming the new growth. Roll the screen up in the daytime.

STAGE 1

year 1, winter

Attach wires to the wall 18 in (45 cm) apart and plant a 1-year-old (maiden) tree without lateral growths 12 in (30 cm) from the wall (see page 11). Train the stem to a cane and cut it back above two strong buds and the first wire.

STAGE 2

year 1, summer

Tie the leader to the vertical cane and tie the two laterals to canes secured at 45°. In late summer, lower them to the first wire.

STAGE 3

year 2, winter

Prune the laterals by one-third to a healthy, downward facing bud. To form the second tier, cut the leader to a bud just above the second wire with two strong buds below it. Cut back any lateral growth beneath the first horizontal to maintain a neat, structured shape.

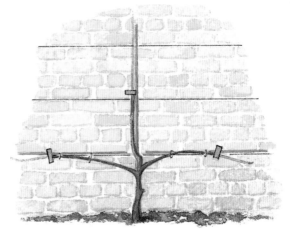

STAGE 4

year 2, summer

Tie the first laterals to the wire and prune shoots on the stems to three leaves above the basal cluster (the group of leaves at the base of the shoot). Attach the shoots of the second tier to canes secured at 45°. Prune any growth on the stem between the first and second tier to three or four leaves. Continue as for the first tier and repeat for the third.

retaining wall

SLOPES IN A GARDEN can present problems. One solution is to make a virtue of them by dividing the garden into different levels using retaining walls. These can be planted up in any number of ways, from grass to highly ornamental displays, and so help to define different parts of the garden. The surface of the wall can also become a decorative feature in its own right, weathering over time with trailing plants growing in nooks and crannies.

materials & equipment

for every 8 ft (2.5 m) of wall
6 cu ft (0.2 cu m) of concrete
½ bag of cement
2 bags of soft sand
6 cu ft (0.2 cu m) of random-size stone blocks (approximately 16–20 blocks)
2 terra-cotta drainage pipes

spade, shovel, wheelbarrow, bricklayer's trowel

for the bed
4 cu ft (0.1 cu m) of broken rocks
4 cu ft (0.1 cu m) of good topsoil or 2 bags of organic material

fork, rake, trowel

plants
see plan opposite

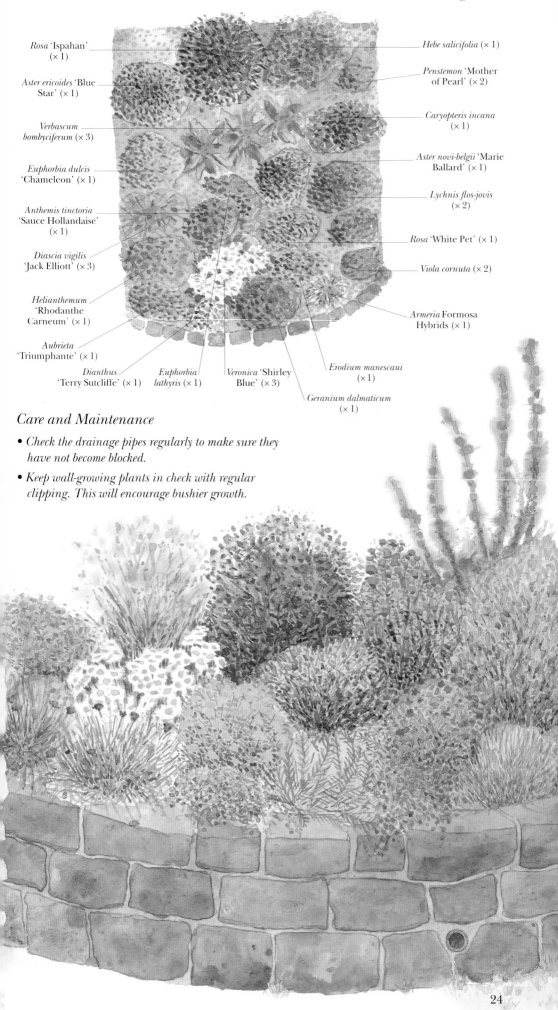

Rosa 'Ispahan'
(× 1)

Aster ericoides 'Blue
Star' (× 1)

Verbascum
bombyciferum (× 3)

Euphorbia dulcis
'Chameleon' (× 1)

Anthemis tinctoria
'Sauce Hollandaise'
(× 1)

Diascia vigilis
'Jack Elliott' (× 3)

Helianthemum
'Rhodanthe
Carneum' (× 1)

Aubrieta
'Triumphante' (× 1)

Dianthus
'Terry Sutcliffe' (× 1)

Euphorbia
lathyris (× 1)

Veronica 'Shirley
Blue' (× 3)

Erodium manescaui
(× 1)

Geranium dalmaticum
(× 1)

Hebe salicifolia (× 1)

Penstemon 'Mother
of Pearl' (× 2)

Caryopteris incana
(× 1)

Aster novi-belgii 'Marie
Ballard' (× 1)

Lychnis flos-jovis
(× 2)

Rosa 'White Pet' (× 1)

Viola cornuta (× 2)

Armeria Formosa
Hybrids (× 1)

Care and Maintenance

• *Check the drainage pipes regularly to make sure they
have not become blocked.*

• *Keep wall-growing plants in check with regular
clipping. This will encourage bushier growth.*

24

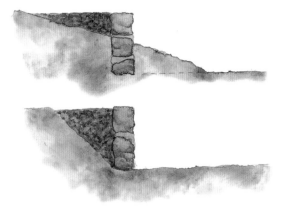

STAGE 1

assessing the site

There are several ways of using a retaining wall on a sloping site. The position of the wall will depend on how you want to redefine the area, minimizing the difference in levels or making a stepped finish as here (left, bottom). Any form of walling can be used: brick, stone, or concrete blocks. A wall that is higher than 18 in (45 cm) should be built by a professional.

STAGE 2

building the foundation

The finished wall will be 12 in (30 cm) high; like all brick and stone walls, it must have a foundation. If the wall is to support an existing bank, as here, dig away some of the bank to allow you to work. Dig a trench 8 in (20 cm) deep along the line of the wall, three times as wide as the final wall will be. Add a 6-in (15-cm) layer of concrete.

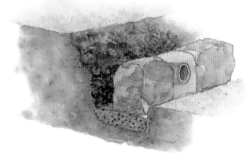

STAGE 3

allowing for drainage

Start building the wall. Just above ground level, insert a short length of pipe and secure it in place so that it is in line with the visible base. This will allow water to seep away and is very important to prevent the bed becoming waterlogged. Add a pipe every 3 ft (1 m). Alternatively, leave spaces between the stones to facilitate drainage.

STAGE 4

constructing the wall

Build above the pipe until the required height is reached. If you plan to include trailing plants in the wall itself, leave a few gaps in the cement-work for planting.

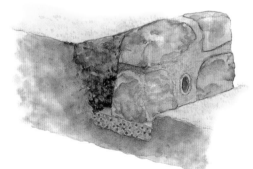

STAGE 5

backfilling with soil

To aid drainage, place a layer of broken rocks between the bed and the wall. Backfill with soil rich in organic matter. If you use the soil that was removed from the bank, avoid putting subsoil near the surface.

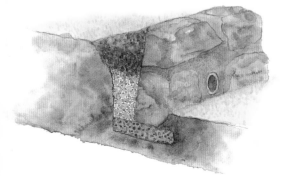

wall cascade

WALLS CAN make a very positive contribution to garden design, especially in a small garden where every inch of space should be used effectively. Decorate them with plants, plaques, containers, or a water feature; the last can range from a simple spout to a cascade and pond, as here. The slate "steps" in this garden have been drilled with outlet holes, but a simple hollow, as used in the project, is just as effective. Plan the feature in advance, finalizing all measurements and proportions.

materials & equipment

foundation
10 55-lb (25-kg) bags of aggregate
2 55-lb (25-kg) bags of cement
6 × 2-ft (180 × 60-cm) sheet of reinforcing mesh
broken stones (multiply the size of the pond by 6 in [15 cm] for the cubic volume of stones required)

walls
5 slabs of slate or cast concrete, 27 × 16 × 2½ in (68 × 40 × 6 cm), slightly dished
enough bricks to build a 4-brick-high wall to the required dimensions
5 55-lb (25-kg) bags of cement
20 55-lb (25-kg) bags of soft sand
16 10 × 12-in (25 × 30-cm) capping slabs

pond
5 × 9-ft (1.5 × 2.7-m) butyl membrane or PVC pond liner
2 5 × 9-ft (1.5 × 2.7-m) sheets of fleece
low-volume submersible pump with its fittings
7-ft (2.2-m) length of ½-in (1-cm) plastic water pipe

spade, shovel, bricklayer's trowel, club hammer, bolster, paintbrush, spirit level, brick-laying line, scissors

STAGE 5

completing the wall

Secure the top slab in the back wall just below the end of the pipe so that the water flows directly onto it. Top the pond wall with capping slabs; these form a decorative finish, provide a surface for plants or for sitting but, above all, hold the pond liner in place.

STAGE 6

adding the pump

Install a submersible pump by following the instructions supplied with the unit. Connect it to the lower end of the pipe where it emerges into the pool, and run the waterproof cable out over one corner at the back of the pool. Hide the cable under plants.

safety

Always employ a professional bricklayer to build tall walls if you lack experience and an electrician to install the pump if you have any doubts.

Care and Maintenance

- *Check periodically that the pump is working effectively, the pipe is clear of debris, and the pond liner is intact and secure.*

STAGE 1

laying the foundation

The whole structure must have a foundation. Dig out the area covered by the walls and pool to a depth of 21 in (53 cm). Fill with 6 in (15 cm) of broken stones or rubble and ram this down. Cover with 12 in (30 cm) of concrete – do not fill to ground level – burying a sheet of reinforcing mesh in the middle of the concrete layer.

STAGE 2

building the walls

Build all the walls two bricks wide. Embed the pipe in the back wall, creating a space by knocking off the inner corners of the bricks along the line of the pipe. The pipe should run from 4 in (10 cm) above the top of the concrete foundation to the point where the water emerges from the wall onto the top slab. When you reach the required height of the pond, stop building and line the pond with garden fleece and then seal it with a pond liner.

STAGE 3

lining the pond

Cover the contours of the pond with the liner and leave 3 in (7.5 cm) to overlap onto the pond wall. Secure the liner into the back wall with capping slabs.

STAGE 4

adding the cascade slabs

Continue to build the back wall and add the slabs at the appropriate intervals. Cement them into the wall to a depth of one row of bricks (left). The slabs should be slightly dished, carved out by a stonemason if slate is used or cast into the concrete. Raise one end of each slab by about 1/4 in (5 mm) to allow the water to run off the other end (left, above).

above Holly (*Ilex aquifolium*) produces an impenetrable, fine-looking hedge with its dark green, shiny leaves.

above Archways in hedges present inviting glimpses of what lies beyond, enticing the viewer to walk through.

above Yew (*Taxus baccata*) creates a wonderfully solid, uniform hedge that makes a perfect backdrop.

hedges can provide far more than a merely functional

boundary between two properties; they can be decorative features in their

own right. They present the possibility of using a wide range of textures and

colors as well as a variety of shapes to enliven a garden.

left and above Compact-growing box (*Buxus sempervirens*) is the perfect shrub for low hedging. It is particularly suitable for creating parterres, where hedges are laid out in formal patterns and filled in with contrasting plants. Such geometric designs can work well even in a small garden, adding classical order. Patience is required when growing box as it makes slow progress; however, once established, it is a reliable, hardy, long-lived plant.

above Yew is a very sculptural material that can be used very successfully to create all manner of topiary. Here, the elegant birds sit above the hedge for greatest impact.

above The versatility of close-growing hedging plants such as yew allows for practical garden features to be created from plants, adding to their charm and interest.

left and below A wide range of shrubs can be used to create informal hedges. These are left largely untrimmed, giving any flower buds a chance to open. Roses, in particular *Rosa rugosa*, are good shrubs to use but other fine flowering hedges are made from lilac, lavender, and hebe. They bring abundance to a garden and often delicious fragrance.

below To relieve the uniformity of a formal hedge, a flowering plant such as this rose can be used to break up the line and color.

formal hedge

FORMAL HEDGES add elegance to a garden, their clean lines bringing an architectural quality to the design. Most formal hedging is relatively slow growing and so does not need much trimming to keep it looking good. Once established, a dense hedge will form an effective windbreak and bring privacy and security to the garden. Yew springs to mind most often when formal hedges are considered, but this beech gives glorious autumn color after the spring greenery.

materials & equipment

1 bucket of organic material per plant
3 beech saplings for the first yd (m) and then 2 per yd (m)
1 stake at either end of the planting then 1 stake for every 6 ft (1.8 m) of hedging

plastic windbreak netting

spade, fork, hoe or rake, garden line, measuring tape, club hammer

training a crenellated top

Most hedges are flat topped or perhaps curved but a much more decorative approach can be used with relative ease. A crenellated finish, like a castle wall, can be trained into the hedge as it grows or cut in at a later stage. If it is cut into a mature hedge, it will take 2 years for the top to green-up.

	FORMAL HEDGING PLANTS	PLANTING DISTANCE	FOLIAGE	TRIMMING TIMES
	Yew (*Taxus baccata*)	24 in (60 cm)	evergreen	twice, summer and autumn
	Golden yew (*T. b.* 'Aurea')	24 in (60 cm)	evergreen	twice, summer and autumn
	Beech (*Fagus sylvatica*)	18 in (45 cm)	deciduous	once, late summer
	Copper beech (*F. s.* 'Atropurpurea')	18 in (45 cm)	deciduous	once, late summer
	Hornbeam (*Carpinus betulus*)	18 in (45 cm)	deciduous	once, mid- to late summer
	Box (*Buxus sempervirens*)	12 in (30 cm)	evergreen	2 or 3 times in the growing season
	Golden box (*B. s.* 'Aureomarginata')	12 in (30 cm)	evergreen	2 or 3 times in the growing season
	Holly (*Ilex aquifolium*)	18 in (45 cm)	evergreen	once, late summer

Care and Maintenance

• *When planting a hedge as a backdrop to a bed, leave at least 12 in (30 cm) between the hedge and the other plants. As with a wall, the area directly beside a hedge can be very dry. The space will also allow access for trimming and inspecting the growth.*

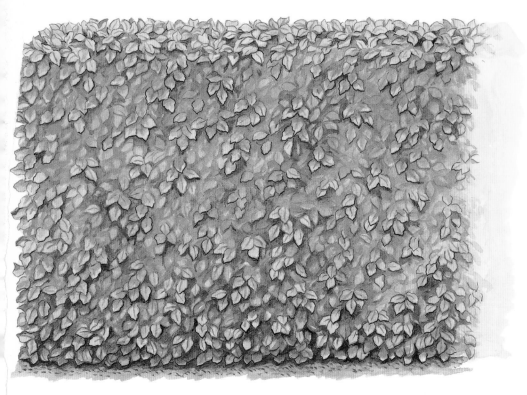

single-row planting

double-row planting

STAGE 1

selecting the right width

Fagus sylvatica, the common beech, is the species to use for a beech hedge. For a narrow or a standard-width hedge, a single row of saplings should be planted 18 in (45 cm) apart. For a thicker hedge, up to 36 in (90 cm) wide, the plants should be staggered in parallel rows, planted 36 in (90 cm) apart within each row with 18 in (45 cm) between the rows.

STAGE 2

planting

Mark out the line of the hedge with a garden line and plant the hedging at the required intervals. The plants should be set to the same depth as they were in the pot or nursery bed.

STAGE 3

using a windbreak

A new hedge will need protection from the effects of a prevailing wind. Knock stakes into the ground at 6-ft (1.8-m) intervals along the length of the windward side of the hedge, 12 in (30 cm) from the plants, and attach plastic windbreak netting. Keep the protection in place until the hedge is established.

STAGE 4

trimming

As the hedge grows, it will need to be clipped or trimmed annually. With an electric trimmer, keep the blade parallel to the hedge and use a wide, sweeping action. A hedge of *Fagus sylvatica* will reach around 10 ft (3 m) in 10 years.

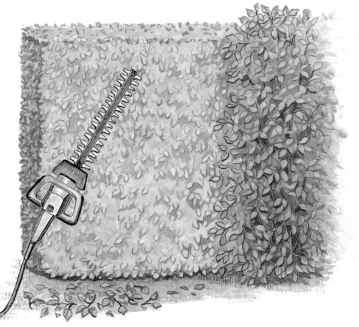

informal hedge

NEATLY CLIPPED hedges are an attractive sight but the other side of
the coin also has enormous appeal. Informal hedges allow shrubs the
freedom to grow and flower and fruit at will. What they lose in neatness
and order they gain in variety and cheerfulness. They bring abundance
to a garden scene and blend into a free-growing scheme. The added
benefit is that informal hedges do not have to be regularly pruned; they
will benefit from such maintenance but can look the part without.

materials & equipment

1 bag of mulch per 7 ft (2.2 m)
1 *Rosa rugosa* plant per 4 ft (1.2 m)

fork, spade, hoe or rake, garden line,
watering can, pruners

alternative hedges

Berberis

Berberis forms a dense, tall hedge and offers year-round interest.
B. darwinii has orange flowers and blue-black fruits while *B. thunbergii*
f. *atropurpurea* has orange flowers and purple foliage, red in autumn.

Berberis darwinii

Berberis thunbergii
f. *atropurpurea*

Hebe

Hedging hebes bear attractive lance-shaped leaves and an
abundance of flowers. They are excellent for coastal gardens.
H. salicifolia has white flowers and *H.* 'Midsummer Beauty' purple.

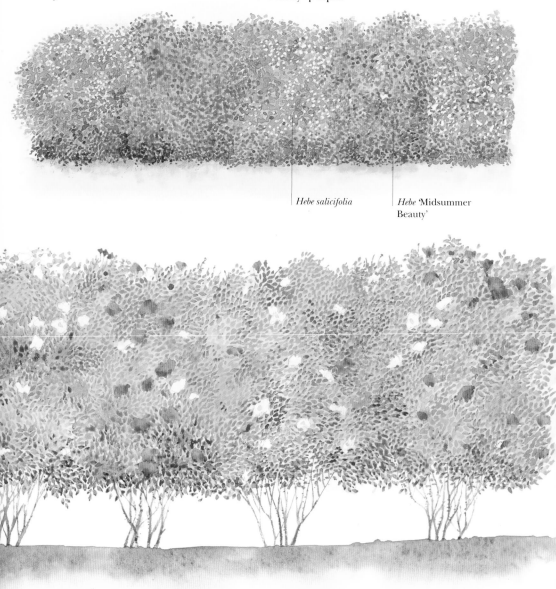

Hebe salicifolia

Hebe 'Midsummer
Beauty'

STAGE 1

appropriate planting

As they grow freely, informal hedges should not be planted close to paths because long branches, especially if thorny as with *Rosa rugosa*, can injure passersby. They are best used as dividers within the garden. Prepare the ground and plant the rose bushes 4 ft (1.2 m) apart.

Rosa rugosa 'Alba'

Rosa rugosa

STAGE 2

young plants

Once planted, water and mulch along the length of the hedge to preserve moisture and keep weeds down. These vigorous roses will quickly fill out.

Care and Maintenance

- *Prune the roses in the same way as a single specimen: in spring, removing dead and diseased wood and reducing main stems by a third and side shoots by two-thirds.*

- *This is not a dense hedge so, although it is thorny, animal-proofing might be advisable. Plant the hedge hard against a fence that, in time, will be hidden by the growth.*

hedge feature

HEDGES CAN BE integrated completely into the garden scene by incorporating a built-in feature that is both practical and decorative. Here, a niche has been carved into a hornbeam hedge to create a secluded and quiet spot for relaxing and contemplating the garden. It is best if the arbor is constructed when the hedge is first laid, for although it is possible to create such a recess by pruning away growth, it will take some years for the cut areas to green over.

materials & equipment

4 hornbeam or beech saplings per yd (m) for each row of the hedge
2 buckets of well-rotted organic material per yd (m)
windbreak netting
1 post per 3 ft (1 m) of netting
staples or string
1 garden bench

spade, pruners, hammer

STAGE 4

completing the arbor

If a seat is placed in the arbor, it is best to use a wooden bench, which can be moved for hedge maintenance, rather than a heavier stone seat.

Care and Maintenance

- *Remove the bench before pruning and check the seat for damage. Use a wood preservative but not creosote, which can harm plants.*
- *Use a sheet to collect hedge clippings to prevent weeds and grass growing up through prunings.*

STAGE 3

completing the framework

Continue to weave in willow sticks, spacing each one 12 in (30 cm) apart, and gradually easing the uprights to meet at a central point. Tie all the sticks together at the top of the frame.

STAGE 4

maintaining the completed cave

The willow sticks will soon root and shoots will extend outward. Encourage these to entwine so that the spaces between the sticks are closed. Prune back growth within the cave.

42

STAGE 1

planting the hedge

Plant a complete row of hornbeam saplings 12 in (30 cm) apart and then plant a second row 18 in (45 cm) away from the first and opposite the spaces between the plants. Leave a gap in the front row of saplings to accommodate the bench.

STAGE 2

pruning the hedge

The hornbeam hedge will reach 10 ft (3 m) in approximately 10 years. As it grows, trim in mid- to late summer, clipping tightly to the stems of the back row within the niche. When the arbor reaches head height, allow the hedge to grow out to the full width. The sides of the arbor should also be tightly clipped.

STAGE 3

caring for the mature hedge

Keep the hedge and the recess neat by pruning annually. Less regular and so more drastic pruning will mean that cut branches and stems will be visible for some time. The top of the arbor can be square as here or, for a softer finish, rounded.

constructing a willow cave

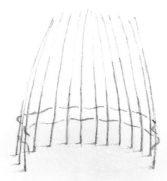

STAGE 1

planting willow sticks

In mid- to late winter, plant a row of 7–8-ft (2.2–2.5-m) tall willow sticks in a semicircle at 10-in (25-cm) intervals. Weave another stick in, 2 ft (60 cm) from the ground, tying it in.

STAGE 2

weaving the framework

Thread another willow stick 2 ft (60 cm) above the first stick, gradually easing the uprights inward into a dome. When you are satisfied with the angle, tie as before.

low hedge

LOW HEDGES are an ideal way of creating internal divisions as well as edging beds. They form a clean line between different areas of the garden often, as here, holding back the abundant growth of a border from a grass path or lawn. The hedge has been further defined by a rim of charming purple-leafed violas. Hedges such as these look best if they are kept trimmed, but slow-growing plants like box require little attention to produce a neat finish.

materials & equipment

plants
12 *Buxus sempervirens* plants per yd (m)
12 *Viola riviniana* plants per yd (m)
plants for the enclosed bed (*see plan opposite*)

fork, spade, trowel, hand-fork, pruners, hedge clippers

pruning template
2 18 × 18-in (45 × 45-cm) pieces of plywood
1 ball of string

planting plan

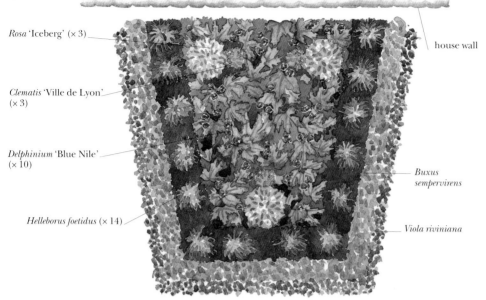

Rosa 'Iceberg' (× 3)

Clematis 'Ville de Lyon' (× 3)

Delphinium 'Blue Nile' (× 10)

Helleborus foetidus (× 14)

house wall

Buxus sempervirens

Viola riviniana

planting the bed

Select plants that will complement the low hedge. This tapering bed is 4 ft (1.2 m) at its widest and 5 ft (1.5 m) long.

Care and Maintenance

- *If trimming the box after planting the violas, remove any cuttings from the bed.*

- *Deadhead the violas regularly to encourage new growth and to maintain a tidy appearance.*

- *Leave the violas over the winter or remove and replace with different low-growing edging plants in the spring.*

46

STAGE 1

planting the hedge

To form a full hedge, the plants must be planted close to each other to cause their foliage to merge, so space the box plants 4 in (10 cm) apart, positioning them close to the edge of the border. They will take 4–5 years to reach 12 in (30 cm) in height.

STAGE 2

making the pruning template

Prune the box hedge in the spring using a template guide for the clippers. Make two plywood frames that will fit exactly over the hedge when it is being trimmed, enabling you to follow the desired shape. Carve away the ends and drill a series of holes at the same point on each frame at the sides and corners and on the top.

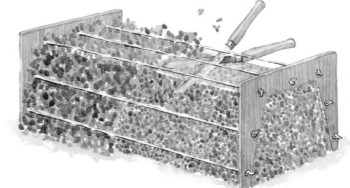

STAGE 3

attaching the template

Thread lengths of string through the holes, knotting them at both ends to secure. Fit both frames over the hedge, pulling the strings tight, and push the frames firmly into the ground.

STAGE 4

trimming

Using the template as a guide, trim the hedge with hand or electric hedge clippers. Remove the template and clear away the clippings.

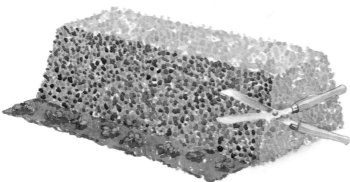

STAGE 5

planting the violas

In spring, plant the violas 4 in (10 cm) apart for a good, tight display. Trim the box during the summer if necessary to keep it neat.

fences

offer the gardener many options. They can provide a highly rustic mood or take on an elegant geometric quality. Trellis and wattle panels come into their own where an internal boundary is needed, and all combine well with plants, be they adjacent beds or scrambling climbers.

above Fences can form a boundary without obscuring the view. Where security is not a problem, a stylish, low, minimalist fence is all that is needed to end a garden.

right The position, size, and all-important design of a gate are significant factors. A double gateway allows greater scope for creativity.

above Trellis is well suited for making garden "rooms." It gives height and can extend across a wide area, enclose a corner, or emphasize a geometric design. And it can become home for climbers – from honeysuckle to roses, jasmine to clematis – or a bold display of nasturtiums.

above A classic feature of many country homes is the crisp, white picket fence, a traditional boundary that justifies its popularity. Fresh, bright posts deserve to be complemented by colorful cottage-garden flowers. Natural wood has a more restrained character while a green or blue stain makes an eye-catching statement.

right This beautiful fence seems to glow from a shady corner. Beyond, tall fronds of lavender echo the blueness of the shade.

above Rustic trellis adds informality with its bark-covered finish and suitability for witty, asymmetrical designs. An excellent screen.

right There are few garden features that add a more rural note than a wattle panel. Originally used by farmers to contain and protect livestock, they now hide unsightly parts of the garden, protect young trees, and create tantalizing passageways to explore.

picket fence

A PICKET FENCE is the ornamental vestige of a defensive palisade in which all the uprights were sharpened to prevent people or animals climbing over. Now the picket fence is a very decorative way of creating a boundary. Its elegant simplicity makes it suitable for formal settings as well as for the exuberance of a cottage garden. Simple flat or pointed pickets are easy to construct, providing the fence is well planned; for more decorative finials, an electric band saw will ease the job.

materials & equipment

foundations
½ bucket of broken rocks per hole
3 buckets of concrete per hole

spade, shovel, spirit level

the fence, per 6½-ft (2-m) section
2 main posts, 5 ft (1.5 m) long and 4 in (10 cm) square, for
the first 6½ ft (2 m) and then 1 per 6½ ft (2 m)
13 pickets, 3½ ft (1.1 m) long and ½ × 3 in (1 × 7.5 cm)
2 rails, 6½ ft (2 m) long and 1½ × 3 in (3 × 7.5 cm)
60 1¾-in (4-cm) galvanized nails

saw, hammer, chisel, measuring tape, ruler, pencil, template
for picket top, spirit level

paintbrushes, primer, undercoat, and top-coat paint,
or exterior wood stain

simple and decorative finials

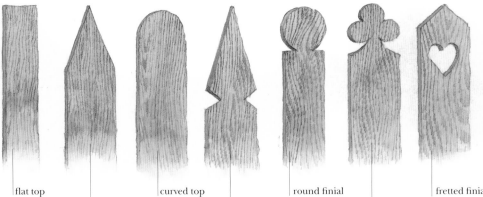

flat top

pointed picket

curved top

spear head

round finial

trifoliate finial

fretted finial

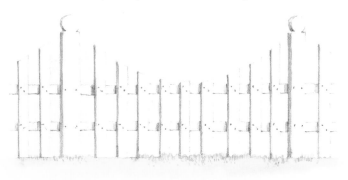

a curved fence

With a little planning, a more elaborate design can be achieved by varying the heights of the pickets and creating a continuous curving finish. The round finials on the posts echo the curve in the picket panels.

a rustic fence

For a highly informal effect, use natural – but not splintered or coarse – wood and simply nail all the parts together. Less precise measurements are needed so the job is more straightforward, but there is still room for a decorative pattern in the pickets.

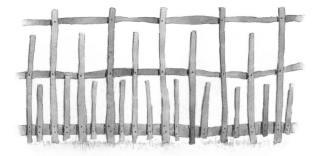

STAGE 1

preparing the main posts

When buying the wood, add 18 in (45 cm) to the length of the posts to secure them in the ground. Work out the position of the picket panel and, with a chisel, make a slot either side of the posts, ⅛ in (3 mm) wider than the bar end. Treat with preservative and position them 4–6½ ft (1.2–2 m) apart.

STAGE 2

securing the main posts

Dig a hole 24 in (60 cm) deep and 10 in (25 cm) square. Fill the bottom with broken rocks, place the post in the hole, and secure the post with concrete. When dry, cover the concrete with soil and turf.

STAGE 3

creating picket panels

Make a template for the picket tops and carve them out. Nail the pickets to the horizontal bars to make panels. Space the pickets 3 in (7.5 cm) apart and position the bars a quarter of the height from the top and bottom. Use galvanized nails as these will not rust.

STAGE 4

securing the panels to the posts

Slot the angled ends of the horizontal bars into the holes on the main post; push in tightly and nail in place. The next post must now be positioned. Dig the foundation and add broken rocks, align the post with the first post, align and secure the picket panel, and fill the foundation hole.

Care and Maintenance

• *Picket fences can be left as natural wood that can last many years, providing the base of the pickets do not touch the ground. Treating the fence with paint or preservative will extend its life; the main posts should always be treated.*

trellis

FREESTANDING TRELLIS is an absolute boon for the gardener. It allows instant screening from the outside world and is ideal for the creation of "rooms" within the garden. Trellis is perfect for supporting climbing plants in their numerous forms, creating a dense screen of foliage and color. This versatile garden structure can also be incorporated into arches, pergolas, or arbors, providing a foothold for plants while allowing light and air through.

materials & equipment

trellis panels
4 × 4-in posts (10 × 10-cm), 12 in (30 cm)
taller than the trellis panels
1 finial per post
½ bucket of broken rocks per hole
3 buckets of dry-mix concrete per hole
4-in (10-cm) galvanized nails
clematis, roses, honeysuckle, or other
climbing plants
plant ties

spade, hammer, spirit level, measuring tape

variations in finials and finishes

Finials are available in different designs, from round to pyramid and spear shaped. These can make a remarkable difference to the finished effect. Finials are simple to fix in place. Trellis can be left as natural wood, painted traditional white, or stained subtle colors such as bluish-green.

Care and Maintenance

- *Prune and train the clematis (see page 99). Both are Group 3 plants, which should be cut right back in early spring.*

- *After pruning, check that the trellis is secure and treat with plant-friendly preservative.*

Stage 1

securing the main post

Freestanding trellis must be bedded firmly in the ground. For the first post, dig a hole 18 in (45 cm) deep and cover the bottom with a 6-in (15-cm) layer of broken rocks. Put the post in the hole, ensuring it is upright, and pack around dry-mix concrete. Cover with soil.

Stage 2

fixing the trellis

Once the main post is solidly in place, nail the first trellis panel to the post using long galvanized nails. Support the far end of the panel at the same time. Align the next post to ensure a neat fit for the trellis and dig the foundation hole.

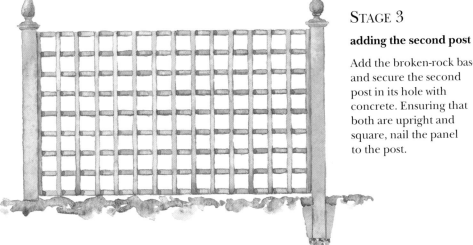

Stage 3

adding the second post

Add the broken-rock base and secure the second post in its hole with concrete. Ensuring that both are upright and square, nail the panel to the post.

Stage 4

completing the trellis

Repeat with the next panel and post and so on until all the trellis is erected. Once the screen is complete, plant the bed in front, here with *Clematis* 'Perle d'Azur' and *C. texensis.*

wattle panels

TO PROVIDE AN attractive temporary screen, there is nothing better than a wattle hurdle. They have a rustic appearance that is particularly effective in less formal settings, and also work well in modern schemes. Their original purpose was to protect and fence in sheep; they can serve a similar function today, keeping pets in or out of a particular part of the garden. Wattle hurdles do not last many years but, providing they are not unstable or dangerous, an aged panel can be picturesque.

materials & equipment

2 6-ft (1.8-m) posts for the first panel and
then 1 per panel
1 wattle panel, 6 × 4 ft (1.8 × 1.2 m), per 6-ft
(1.8-m) run
galvanized wire

spade, spirit level, pliers

a temporary windbreak

Wattle panels make effective windbreaks while a new hedge is growing. Position them about 3 ft (1 m) away from the young plants so they still get the light. The panels should withstand the wind but do check them periodically.

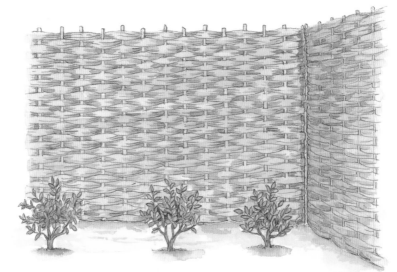

a garden screen

Wattle panels can be used as a screen to hide ugly but necessary features such as trash cans and compost heaps. Position the panels so that access is easy, and allow plenty of room to maneuver for emptying cans or collecting compost. Use a third wire tie to secure the panels as the structure is likely to be knocked in such a position.

an open wattle fence

This effective fence is easy to make. Hammer stakes into the ground 12 in (30 cm) apart and weave wands of willow or hazel between them, three or four wands in each directions, twisted to form two "ropes." Ideal for an internal screen.

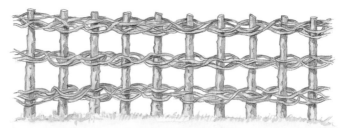

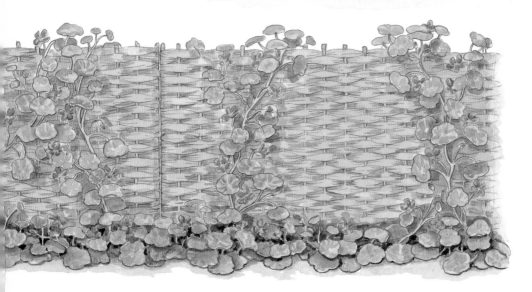

securing the panel: visible posts

For a fairly long-term panel, secure posts into the ground (see page 51). For a temporary screen, the posts can be held firm with rammed earth. Wind heavy galvanized wire around the posts and through the panels 4 in (10 cm) from the top and bottom of the panel.

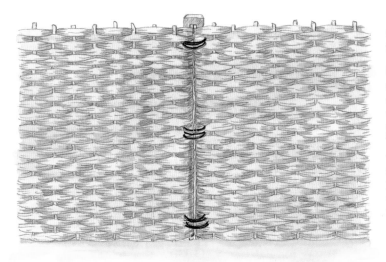

securing the panel: invisible posts

Secure the posts as above and bring the edges of the panels together in front of the posts, hiding them. Work the galvanized wire around the post and both panels. Do not leave the end of the wire exposed as this can be dangerous.

Care and Maintenance

- *Untreated wattle panels will last 10 years at the most. Treated with a preservative – although not creosote, which can harm plants – they will last much longer.*

- *In windy situations, use a third length of wire to secure the panels to the posts (above).*

- *Check that the posts are secure, particularly where only rammed earth has been used.*

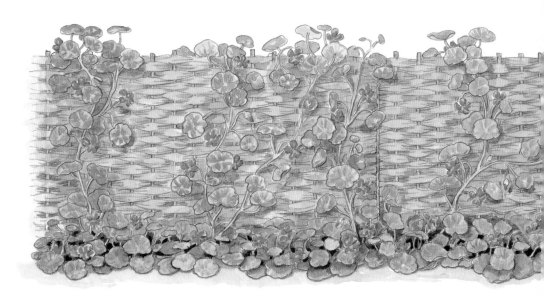

rustic trellis

RUSTIC TRELLIS has a romantic look that always lifts a garden design. The wood has not been machined and is pleasingly irregular in thickness and shape. The structure can be covered with plants, but if a more restrained covering is preferred, rustic trellis is ideal as it is attractive in its own right. The trellis is available ready-made but it is very simple to make – it does not require advanced carpentry skills – and making your own allows you to tailor the design to your exact needs.

materials & equipment

foundations
½ bucket of broken rocks per hole
3 buckets of concrete per hole

spade, shovel, spirit level

the trellis, per 6-ft (1.8-m) section
2 poles for uprights, 8 ft (2.5 m) long and 4–5 in
(10–12.5 cm) across, for the first section and then
1 per section
2 poles for crossbars, 8 ft (2.5 m) long and 3–4 in
(7.5–10 cm) across
3 poles for struts, 3 ft (1 m) long and 3–4 in
(7.5–10 cm) across
4-in (10-cm) galvanized nails
wood preservative

saw, hammer, chisel, measuring tape, old paintbrush

planting plan

Plants suitable for climbing over rustic trellising include clematis, climbing and rambling roses, honeysuckle, and grape vines. The trellis needs to look balanced, so complementary plants should be selected to grow beneath the structure. This scheme is 6 × 4 ft (1.8 × 1.2 m).

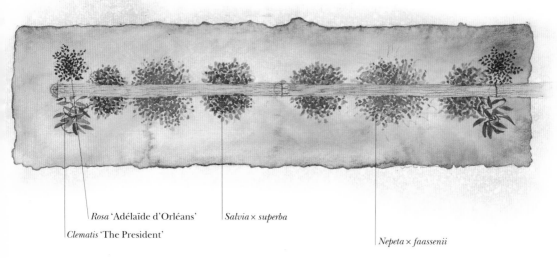

Rosa 'Adélaïde d'Orléans'   *Salvia* × *superba*

Clematis 'The President'

Nepeta × *faassenii*

Care and Maintenance

- *If the whole trellis is treated with preservative (not just the areas of the main posts that are sunk into the ground), the life of the structure will be extended. Do not use creosote as this can harm plants.*

- *After the winter, check that the trellis is secure and replace any decayed parts.*

- *The clematis is a Group 2 plant and so should be pruned lightly (see page 99).*

- *Do not prune the rose in the first year. Thereafter, each year remove two or three whole stems after flowering, cut back the remaining stems by a quarter, and reduce the side shoots by two-thirds.*

STAGE 1

the posts and the crossbar

Secure the posts (see page 51), first stripping the bark from the section that is to be held in the ground and treating it with preservative. Once the posts are firm, attach the crossbar using simple halved joints (where half the thickness is removed) and long galvanized nails.

STAGE 2

the second crossbar

The most important joints are those where struts meet the main upright posts. A simple niche can be cut into the post to correspond with the pointed end of the crossbar. Do not cut too far into the post as this will weaken it. Secure the wood with long nails.

STAGE 3

the central strut

For decorative elements, little in the way of true jointing is required. One piece of wood is simply butted up against another and held in place with nails.

STAGE 4

the diagonal bars

The diagonal bars are useful for training climbers. Measure the bars well, make right-angled ends, and secure them into the framework with nails.

gateway

GATEWAYS TO GARDENS and through fences or hedges within gardens are a standard feature. External gateways set the tone of a garden design as they are the first thing encountered upon arrival. Internal gates and arches are also integral to a scheme, announcing the beginning of another area. Such features should draw both the eyes and feet of visitors. Gateways should not only be decorative in their own right but should also frame what lies beyond, creating an enticing vista.

materials & equipment

foundations
½ bucket broken rocks per hole
3 buckets concrete per hole

gateway
4 6½-ft (2-m) lengths of 1 × 5-in
(2.5 × 12.5-cm) timber
2 8-ft (2.5-m) lengths of 1 × 8-in
(2.5 × 20-cm) timber
130 ft (39 m) of ¾ × 1½-in
(2 × 3-cm) timber batten
110 ft (33 m) of ½ × ¾-in (1 × 2-cm)
timber batten
1¼-in (3-cm) galvanized nails

gate
50 ft (15 m) of 1 × 2-in (2.5 × 5-cm)
timber
10 ft (3 m) of 1 × 3-in
(2.5 × 7.5-cm) timber
1½-in (3-cm) galvanized nails
pair of 10-in (25-cm) strap hinges
gate latch
screws

paintbrushes, primer, undercoat, and
top-coat paint, or exterior wood stain

measuring tape, large sheet of paper,
brown tape, pencil, hammer, saw,
chisel, carpenter's square, wood glue

STAGE 6

preparing the gate

Cut the gate pickets from 1 × 2-in (2.5 × 5-cm) timber. Calculate the differing lengths of the wood by using the curved template for the top of the gateway. Carve the picket spikes and smooth the wood. Loosely tack the pickets to a cross bar to mark the height and width of the gate; it must be ½ in (1 cm) narrower than the gateway arch to allow for a gap on either side when hanging.

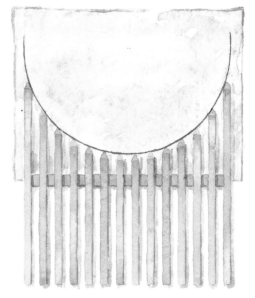

STAGE 7

constructing the gate

Permanently fix the gate using 1 × 3-in (2.5 × 7.5-cm) timber for the cross braces and galvanized nails.

STAGE 8

hanging and painting

Hang the gate with strap hinges on the preferred side of the arch so that it opens outward and add a latch. Paint the whole structure with a primer, undercoat, and then at least one top coat. Alternatively, use a wood stain. When the finish is dry, plant the adjacent beds.

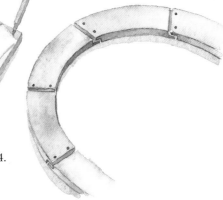

STAGE 1

making a template

Make a template of the curved top of the arch by drawing it on a large sheet of paper, joining several sheets together if necessary.

STAGE 2

making the gateway arch

Using the template, cut the upright sections of the arch from 1 × 5-in (2.5 × 12.5-cm) timber. Then cut and join the arched sections in at least four pieces as described on page 94. Make two identical arches in this way.

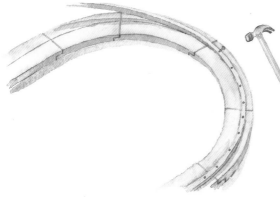

STAGE 3

completing the arches

Draw a line 2 in (5 cm) in from the outer edge around the inside of the arch and nail a ¾ × 1½-in (2 × 3-cm) batten along this line. Again, repeat on the second arched section.

STAGE 4

erecting the arches

Dig four holes 24 in (60 cm) deep for the legs of the arch. Ram 6 in (15 cm) of broken rocks into the bottom of each. Position the arches so they are set at the same level, upright and the correct distance apart, and pour 15 in (38 cm) of concrete around each leg.

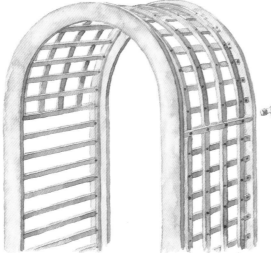

STAGE 5

making the trellis

Cut and nail ¾ × 1½-in (2 × 3-cm) battens horizontally between the main limbs of the arch onto the outside of the lining strips, allowing 4 in (10 cm) between each. When complete, nail the ½ × ¾ in (1 × 2 cm) battens vertically around the outside of the horizontal strips at 4-in (10-cm) intervals to form the trellis. Use separate pieces for the curved top and nail an extra horizontal batten across the outside of the joins.

above A trellis-pillar gives distinction to the corner of a garden shelter; the roses draw you closer.

above Shapes and textures work together in a stepped path, given softness by the pergola-style arches.

above A stream marks a clear divide in a garden, whether architectural and orderly or informal and lush.

decorative dividers are the wealth of

screens and edgings, boundaries and barriers that do not conform to the standard forms. Pleached trees can march across a garden or hazel rods delineate a border. A rose-covered archway can curve over a path or a row of sunflowers can bring delight one year, to be replaced by runner beans the next. Illusion even plays its part, mirrors revealing a scene that is not there.

above Strongly trained and structured fruit trees can form a decorative screen.

right Smaller touches can make a surprising difference in the garden. Edging hurdles bring a note of order to abundant growth.

above The curious structure of pleached trees is best seen during the winter when their highly pruned, twiggy branches stand out starkly.

left An orchard in bloom. The row of trees is grouped with lines of irises and rose bushes and a swathe of tulips. The spring flowers bring gaiety to the order.

below Given space, a single pleached tree can form a boundary. Here, ranked specimens are both strange and impressive.

plant screen

WHILE BOUNDARIES that mark the perimeters of a garden are likely
to be permanent, there is no reason why those within the garden
should not change from time to time, both in position and in
composition. Unsupported tall annuals such as sunflowers are perfect
for such a divider. Their flowers add a touch of brightness and gaiety to
the boundary while their foliage provides a more solid screen. Grow
plants from seed for an inexpensive display that can change yearly.

materials & equipment

planting
enough seed to produce at least 20 *Tropaeolum majus*
enough seed to produce at least 20 *Helianthus annuus* 'Velvet Queen'

40 pots
potting media

an alternative screen

Any tall annual, biennial, or perennial will provide a colorful boundary. These can be combined with smaller plants for ground-level interest. Here, a 4-ft (1.2-m)-tall dahlia is combined with mid-height California poppy (*Eschscholzia californica*) and dwarf pot marigolds (*Calendula officinalis*). Plant them in meandering rows after the last frost, the dahlias 18 in (45 cm) apart, the other plants 12 in (30 cm) apart.

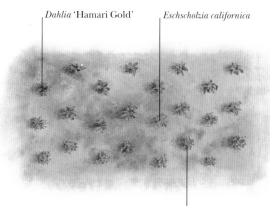

Dahlia 'Hamari Gold'

Eschscholzia californica

Calendula officinalis 'Fiesta Gitana'

STAGE 1

sunflower seedlings

Sow sunflower and nasturtium seeds in pots in mid-spring. The seedlings can be planted out once the threat of frost has passed.

Helianthus annuus 'Velvet Queen'

Tropaeolum majus

STAGE 2

planting out

Thoroughly dig the bed and add well-rotted organic material. Plant the sunflower seedlings in two parallel rows 24 in (60 cm) apart. Within each row, the sunflowers should be planted at 18-in (45-cm) intervals (single stem varieties, as opposed to this branching variety, should be 12 in [30 cm] apart). Plant the nasturtiums outside the rows of sunflowers, staggered between them. The nasturtiums will grow freely up and around the sunflowers, giving color to the base of the screen.

STAGE 3

the mature screen

The sunflower *Helianthus annuus* 'Velvet Queen' will reach 5 ft (1.5 m) in height and flowers from late summer to early autumn. It will do well in partial shade as well as full sun (the flowers will turn to the sun) and does not need to be staked except on a windy site. The nasturtiums will scramble up and through the sunflowers. The whole screen will die back during the autumn.

rose arch

ARCHES CAN BE put to very good use in the garden, dividing one area from another, but their greatest asset is that they are ideal for growing climbers. Arches entice you to pass through and your reward with this example would be the fragrance of the rambling rose. Wooden archways can be made from scratch but a variety of elegant metal and wooden frames are readily available in easy-assemble kit form, so any garden can be given a passageway and a home for delightful climbers.

materials & equipment

foundations
½ bucket of broken rocks per hole
3 buckets of concrete per hole

spade, shovel, spirit level

planting
2 *Rosa* 'Adélaïde d'Orléans' plants
1 bucket of organic material per plant

spade, fork, pruners, plant ties

alternative uses

Rose arches are used as romantic and fragrant "doorways" from one part of a garden to another, usually covering a path. They can mark a gateway through a wall or a hedge or crown the top of steps, while a series of arches creates a "pergola" effect, which can be very dramatic.

framing a garden door   **marking a rise of steps**   **arching across a path**

Care and Maintenance

- *Before planting, treat the metal framework with a preservative that will not harm the roses.*
- *Inspect the structure during the winter.*

selecting an arch

The arch must be wide enough to walk through when it is covered with roses. The flowers can extend 12 in (30 cm) into the arch from the sides and the top.

STAGE 1

securing the foundation

In sheltered positions it is sufficient to ram the earth down around the legs to stabilize an arch, but on exposed sites it must be well secured as winds combined with the weight of plants could topple the structure. Check the manufacturer's recommended depth for sinking the arch. Ideally, for a larger arch, you should dig a hole 24 in (60 cm) deep and 8 in (20 cm) square for each leg, fill the bottom of the holes with 6 in (15 cm) of broken rocks, and sink the arch 18 in (45 cm) into the ground. Check that the arch is straight, and secure with concrete, leaving the last 2 in (5 cm) to be covered with soil.

STAGE 2

planting roses

Plant a climbing or rambling rose on either side – here the rambler *Rosa* 'Adélaïde d'Orléans' – on the outside of the arch, away from any concrete or rammed-earth foundations. Lead the stems, with a cane if necessary, onto the arch and tie the branches in.

STAGE 3

pruning

Prune as for climbing roses on a wall (see pages 11–12), but train them up over the arch rather than fanning them out. Tie in any wandering shoots but do not allow the climbers to become too thick. Take care to remove all dead wood.

pleached trees

FOR A GRAND touch in the garden, a boundary or avenue of pleached
trees can be very striking. A dramatic feature of large, formal grounds,
they can work well in a smaller garden because the trees are kept
clipped and so will not dominate the space. The idea is to create a
"wall" of trees; two rows make an avenue and these can be trained
together to form a tunnel. It does not take long to create a mature
display; this boundary has taken only five years to grow.

materials & equipment

framework, per 10-ft (3-m) section
2 poles, 10 ft (3 m) long and 4–5 in (10–12.5 cm) across, for
the first section and then 1 per section
4 12-ft (3.7-m) lengths of galvanized wire per section
8 1-in (2.5-cm) galvanized staples per section

spade, hammer, spirit level, measuring tape

planting
1 bucket of organic material per tree
plant ties
1 *Tilia platyphyllos* plant per pole

spade, pruners

STAGE 3

pruning, year 2 or 3, winter

Continue to tie in side branches to the wires as they grow and, when the branches from different trees meet, interlace them. When the main stem reaches the top of the post, prune it back just above a pair of side shoots. Cut back all side shoots to three buds. Pinch out any unwanted growth.

STAGE 4

pruning, year 4, winter

Remove any branches that grow beyond the framework by cutting back to a bud. As the stems produce new growth, weave the smaller, pliable shoots through the main stems so that you have a dense coverage along each tier. Continue to prune and train in this way each winter. The posts and wires can be removed after 5 years or once the trees are well established. Cut the posts at the base if necessary.

STAGE 1

constructing the framework

Use strong posts that can be sunk 24 in (60 cm) into the ground, leaving enough length above to reach the required height of the trees. Secure them with rammed earth, 8–10 ft (2.5–3 m) apart. Stretch galvanized wire along the posts starting at 4 ft (1.2 m) and at 2-ft (60-cm) intervals. Loop the wire around the posts, securing it with metal staples. Trim the wire on the end posts.

STAGE 2

planting and pruning, year 1

Lime, particularly *Tilia platyphyllos* as here, and hornbeam (*Carpinus*) are the best trees for pleaching. Plant a 3- or 4-year-old tree in front of each post at any time from mid-autumn to early spring. Tie the main stem to the post and the main branches to the wires. Cut back any stems that are growing below the level of the wire and any that are growing outward.

sweet-pea divider

UNLIKE FIXED FEATURES such as hedges and walls, temporary dividers mean the gardener can move elements around and alter the shape of a design. Such temporary displays can also be used as screens while a permanent feature, such as a tree, is growing. Many plants can be used to make a divider; brightly colored summer flowers such as sweet peas can completely change the appearance of a garden, proving so successful that they can become an annual feature.

materials & equipment

for a 10-ft (3-m) run
2 wooden pegs
ball of string
3 8-ft (2.5-m) stakes
12 peasticks
1 bag of organic material

spade or fork, rake, trowel, pruners, club hammer

plants
Lathyrus odoratus (12 plants or a packet of seed)

alternative supports

A row of canes can be used to support climbing plants such as runner beans. Push the poles or canes firmly into the ground at 12-in (30-cm) intervals and tie one across the top to steady the structure. This will make an ideal support for the decorative bean plants.

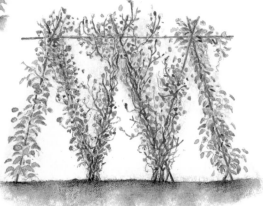

a bamboo chevron

A striking geometric support can be made using medium-size canes to form a chevron pattern. Place one cane horizontally across the top for stability. Many decorative climbers will enjoy trailing over this framework.

other decorative climbers

Clematis, jasmine, and honeysuckle prefer to roam freely over any structure. The deciduous woody-stemmed plants shown below produce fragrant flowers to add to their decorative qualities.

Ipomoea hederacea　　*Clematis 'Perle d'Azur'*　　*Tropaeolum peregrinum*　　*Thunbergia alata*

STAGE 1

preparing

Buying seed is cheaper than buying plants and it gives you the chance to select colors. Sow the seed in a tray in the early winter, placing the container in a warm place, 64–66°F (18–19°C). Once seedlings have sprouted, prick them out and plant on into small pots and water well. When the plants grow, pinch out the first shoots so that the sweet peas produce more flowers.

STAGE 2

creating the divider

Push the peasticks (a central branch with numerous supple twigs) into the ground, 10 in (25 cm) apart. Encourage the twigs to entwine, particularly at the top of the branches as this will provide a better support for the plants' tendrils.

STAGE 3

making a support

If the position is exposed, knock a strong stake 18 in (45 cm) into the ground about every 6 ft (1.8 m) and thread two strings through the peasticks, using the stakes as more solid supports. Plant the sweet peas along the base of the row, 10 in (25 cm) apart.

STAGE 4

maintaining

Tie in stems as they grow. If you pick flowers on a regular basis, you will have a more luxuriant crop of sweet peas. Prune out flowers as they fade; this stops them setting seed, which would reduce flowering. Once the sweet peas have finished flowering, remove the plants, the sticks, and the stakes.

miniature hurdles

DECORATIVE EDGING adds a finishing touch to borders and paths, defining the boundary between one area and another. An edging can also serve other, practical functions; here, the charming miniature hurdles hold back the plants from the lawn and deter pets from running into the border. Canes can do the same job but they are far less attractive. These decorative hurdles can be bought or they are simple to make – an excellent project for the novice carpenter!

materials & equipment

For each hurdle
2 sweet chestnut uprights, 9 in (23 cm) long and 2 in (5 cm) across
5 sweet chestnut crossbars, 16 in (40 cm) long and 1 in (2.5 cm) across
3 sweet chestnut braces, 8 in (20 cm) long and 1 in (2.5 cm) across
galvanized nails

hammer, drill, sharp knife, chisel

an alternative edging

The simplest form of temporary edging is to make hazel hoops. Use thin, pliable hazel rods about 3 ft (1 m) long, push one end into the soil, and then carefully bend the rod over. Overlap the rods for an elegant, effective finish.

Care and Maintenance

- *Apply a wood preservative that will not harm plants.*
- *Periodically check the hurdles for damage, and repair or replace any affected parts.*
- *Remove the hurdles in the winter, repair any damage, apply a preservative, and store them in a dry place.*

STAGE 1

preparing the wood

These hurdles are made from sweet chestnut but hazel can also be used. Strip off the bark and split the stems in half lengthways with a knife and chisel.

STAGE 2

preparing the parts

Cut the uprights and crossbars to length. Make a pointed end at the bottom of the uprights and drill five holes through each, starting 2 in (5 cm) from the top and spacing them 2 in (5 cm) apart. Shave the ends of the crossbars to fit into the holes.

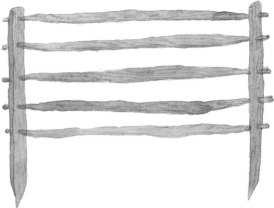

STAGE 3

assembling the hurdle

Put the hurdle together and drill small pilot holes horizontally through the uprights and ends of the crossbars. Secure the structure by carefully hammering small galvanized nails through the pilot holes.

STAGE 4

attaching the bars

Cut the central upright bar and the two diagonals to length, position them, drill pilot holes, and secure with galvanized nails. The hurdle now has the appearance of a miniature five-bar gate.

STAGE 5

positioning hurdles

The secret to using hurdles is to position them before the plants begin to grow. They will restrain excessive growth but some stems and leaves will grow over and through the hurdles, giving them a natural look. Simply push the hurdles into the soil. In packed soil, pilot holes will help.

trompe l'oeil

BOUNDARIES CAN BE confining, especially in small gardens. However, it is possible to extend your prospect without making your garden larger simply by deceiving the eye. Well planned and executed, trompe l'oeil will give the impression that the garden continues beyond the fixed perimeters, apparently revealing more plants and interest through a window or gateway. A scene that complements the style and scale of your garden can be painted in durable paints or, more simply, a mirror can be used, as here, to reflect parts of the real garden.

materials & equipment

mirror
3½ × 6½-ft (1.1 × 2-m) mirror
3½ × 6½-ft (1.1 × 2-m) sheet of cardboard
mirror plates

arch template
2 8 × 4-ft (2.5 × 1.2-m) sheets of chipboard
6 × 4-ft (1.8 × 1.2-m) sheet of hardboard

brickwork
2 cu ft (0.05 cu m) of concrete
80 bricks
2 55-lb (25-kg) bags of cement
8 55-lb (25-kg) bags of soft sand

trellis
7-ft (2.2-m) length of 2 × 6-in (5 × 15-cm) timber
2 10-ft (3-m) lengths of 2 × 8-in (5 × 20-cm) timber
80 ft (25 m) of 2 × 4-in (5 × 10-cm) timber
3-ft (1-m) length of ½-in (1-cm) wooden dowel
150 ft (45 m) of 1 × ½-in (2.5 × 1-cm) wooden battens
1 lb (500 g) of ¾-in (2-cm) galvanized nails

large sheet of paper, pencil, string, measuring tape, brown tape, spade, shovel, bricklayer's trowel, spirit level, hammer, band saw, drill, ½-in (1-cm) drill bit, chisel, square, paintbrush, wood glue, exterior wood stain

STAGE 6

making the trellis arch

Use the length of 2 × 6-in (5 × 15-cm) wood for the trellis arch. Cut it into three sections. Place these in turn on different parts of the arch, overlapping each section slightly, and draw the relevant curve on the wood. Make a parallel line 2 in (5 cm) deep and cut the piece out.

STAGE 7

putting the arch together

Make halved joints in the ends of the wood (see page 103), and glue and dowel them together in a continuous curve.

STAGE 8

completing the trellis arches

Draw the larger curves for the outer pieces on a large sheet of paper. Use the 2 × 8-in (5 × 20-cm) wood to form the arches as described above. Lay the arches on the ground and join them to the uprights. Add the top rail and nail the battens diagonally onto the back of the frame. Stain the trellis with exterior wood stain.

STAGE 9

securing the trellis

Get help to raise the trellis and fix it to the wall using blocks of wood to maintain a gap between trellis and wall.

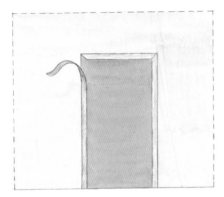

STAGE 1

securing the mirror

Fix the mirror in the center of a 10 × 20-ft (3 × 6-m) wall with mirror plates. Protect it by covering it with heavy cardboard, taped round the edges. (When the structure is complete, the cardboard can be cut away around the arch, leaving the remainder behind the brickwork.)

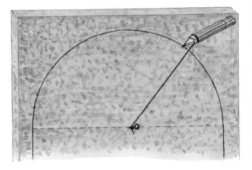

STAGE 2

marking out the template

Cut two sheets of chipboard to the shape and size of the finished arch. Use a pencil and string to mark out the top of the arch from a measured center point.

STAGE 3

making the template

Spacing the two sheets 4¼ in (11 cm) apart, nail a sheet of hardboard around the profile to make a solid structure on which to build the brickwork.

STAGE 4

preparing foundations and erecting the template

Dig two holes for the foundations, 12 × 8 × 12 in (30 × 20 × 30 cm) deep, and fill with concrete to within 2 in (5 cm) of ground level. Position the template and, using a spirit level, make certain that it is perfectly upright.

STAGE 5

building the arch

Build up the brickwork, using the template for a symmetrical finish and to support the arch as it is built. The final, center bricks or keystones will have to be cut to a wedge shape to fit the curved space. When the cement has hardened (in 2–3 days), remove the template, cutting it into sections if necessary.

basic techniques

LIVING BOUNDARIES

GROUND PREPARATION

To get the best results from any plants, it is essential to prepare the ground thoroughly. Remove all perennial weeds either by digging and removing by hand or by using weed killers, carefully following the instructions for the product. If possible, leave the ground fallow for at least six months and remove any weeds that reappear. Prepare the soil in the early autumn and plant in the spring.

digging

Dig the ground; if it is heavy, break up the soil below the top layer with a fork and work organic material into this. The addition of large quantities of organic material will improve the structure of the soil, will provide nutrients for the plants, and will help to preserve moisture around the roots of the plants. Methodical double digging can pay great dividends for the future health and productivity of a bed so is well worth the effort involved. Do not dig if the ground is wet and, once the double digging has been completed, leave the area to allow winter frosts and rain to break down the soil and kill pests. Avoid walking on the area during this time as it can compact the soil.

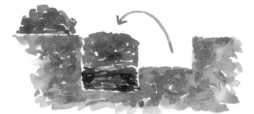

2 *Work the trench for a further 12 in (30 cm) and add organic material. Dig out the next trench and use the earth to fill the first.*

3 *As before, work through the layer below, breaking up the ground with a fork and adding organic material. Continue to work in this way.*

double digging
1 *Dig a trench, 12–18 in (30–45 cm) wide and 12 in (30 cm) deep. Save the removed earth.*

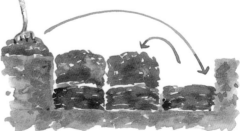

4 *When you have reached the end of the border, fill the final trench with the earth removed from the first trench.*

drainage

Other than those native to marshland or water, plants do not like to be waterlogged, so, if water lies in the soil, it is important to install some form of drainage system such as digging a ditch or laying land drains. The most appropriate approach will depend on the site and the plants. Grit should also be added to the soil to help water seep through.

drainage systems
An effective drainage system can be created by digging a hole 4–6 ft (1.2–1.8 m) deep and adding broken stones topped with good-quality soil.

A shallower hole of 24 in (60 cm) will be effective if tile drains are used in a herringbone pattern. These should be angled downward.

SOIL CONDITIONERS

Chipped or composted bark Best used as a mulch

Commercially prepared conditioners Good conditioners but expensive

Farmyard manure Good all-around conditioner as long as it does not contain weed seed

Garden compost Good all-around conditioner as long as it does not contain weed seed

Leaf mulch Excellent conditioner and mulch

Peat Little nutrient value and breaks down too quickly to be of great value

Seaweed Excellent conditioner as it includes plenty of minerals

Spent hops Good conditioner but limited nutrients

Spent mushroom compost Good conditioner and mulch but includes lime

---

organic material

Organic material is important for all gardens as a soil conditioner, as a nutrient for growing plants, and as a mulch to help preserve moisture and keep weeds down. The cheapest way to obtain it is to make your own compost by rotting down any weed-seed-free garden waste such as old herbaceous stems, flower heads, and grass mowings. Woody material will need to be shredded first. Any uncooked vegetable waste such as peelings from the kitchen can also be used. Make a compost bin, preferably with at least two sections. A similar bin should be used for composting autumn leaves as leaf mold makes an excellent mulch. Farmyard manure is also a very useful addition to the soil as long as it does not contain weed-seed.

compost bin
A compost bin should have at least two compartments, one for new material that is rotting down, the other for current use.

planting

Most climbers are now sold in containers and can be planted at any time of the year, providing the weather is not too hot, cold, or dry and as long as they are kept watered and protected from strong winds. Bare-rooted plants or those that have been moved should be planted during the winter. Prepare the ground thoroughly, preferably well in advance. Dig in some slow-release fertilizer and dig the hole.

It is usually very dry next to a wall or fence, so always plant climbers at least 12 in (30 cm) away from the boundary, using one or more canes to guide the stems into the wires or other support. Most climbing plants should be planted at the same depth as they were in their pots, indicated by the soil ring around the stem. The exception is clematis, which should be planted 2–3 in (5–7.5 cm) deeper.

Water the plant well and mulch with well-rotted organic material such as leaf mold or garden compost. Clematis like to have their roots cool so, if possible, either plant another shrub nearby to keep the sun off the soil around the roots or cover the ground with stone slabs or tile.

CLIMBERS

It is essential to understand the climbing and clinging method of a particular plant to know whether it will be successful in a given location. This knowledge will enable you to provide the most suitable support for the plant.

clinging: ivy
Clinging climbers need no additional support on a wall or fence as they creep up the structure, hugging close to the surface.

tendrils: clematis
Where tendrils are produced specifically for encircling a support, the plant will do well with a wire framework or climbing over another plant.

twining: honeysuckle
Plants that twine do best with a wirework support or trellis. Growth can be assisted by directing shoots to a bare area of the support.

scrambling: rambling or climbing roses
In the wild, such plants would scramble over trees and shrubs. They lean upon their support so, in cultivation, need to be tied to a structure.

PRUNING AND MAINTAINING CLIMBERS

maintenance

The sheer weight of an untended climber can damage a support while overcrowding can adversely affect flower production. Pruning ensures an attractive framework and promotes vigorous growth and plentiful flowers. With these issues in mind, it is advisable to prune all climbing plants, even if it is only to cut out dead wood.

roses

Climbing and rambling roses can be very vigorous. They create excellent cover but benefit enormously from pruning and training. Climbing roses can be pruned in the autumn or winter while rambling roses should be pruned after flowering, in late summer. Deadheading assists growth but should not be carried out if you want hips.

pruning a climbing rose
Do not prune during the first year. After that, only prune main shoots if they grow beyond their allotted space, but prune side shoots by two-thirds.

pruning a rambling rose
Do not prune during the first year. After that, remove two or three whole stems each year (it is easier to remove them in sections), and cut back the remaining main stems by a third and side shoots by two-thirds.

While problematic because of thorns, untying roses from the wall, fence, or trellis and laying them on the ground makes pruning much easier. When all the unwanted material has been removed, the stems should be retrained onto the support, preferably in curving arches as this will promote flowering and presents a very pleasing, open pattern.

clematis

Pruning clematis is a little complicated as different plants need different treatment. There are three groups and it is essential to know which group a specimen belongs to to avoid destructive or insufficient pruning. Correct pruning will encourage full growth and maximum flowering.

group 1
Early-flowering species that flower on the previous year's shoots: only prune out dead material. If you do not want the plant to become too large and heavy, remove a few stems each year. Prune plants during the autumn.

group 2
Large-flowered varieties that flower early to mid-season on new shoots from the previous year's stems: prune old wood lightly in early spring.

group 3
Large-flowered varieties that flower late on new wood: these can be cut right back, cutting just above a strong pair of buds. It looks brutal but they will grow all the stronger for this treatment. Prune in early spring.

EXAMPLES OF CLEMATIS AND THEIR GROUP	
C. 'Abundance' 3	C. 'Jackmanii' 3
C. alpina 1	C. 'Lasurstern' 2
C. armandii 1	C. 'Little Nell' 3
C. 'Barbara Dibley' 2	C. macropetala 1
C. 'Barbara Jackman' 2	C. 'Marie Boisselot' 2
C. 'Bill MacKenzie' 3	C. 'Miss Bateman' 2
C. cirrhosa 1	C. montana 1
C. 'Comtesse de Bouchaud' 3	C. 'Mrs. Cholmondeley' 2
C. 'Countess of Lovelace' 2	C. 'Nelly Moser' 2
C. 'Daniel Deronda' 2	C. 'Niobe' 2
C. 'Doctor Ruppel' 2	C. 'Perle d'Azur' 3
C. 'Duchess of Albany' 3	C. 'Rouge Cardinal' 3
C. 'Elsa Späth' 2	C. 'Royal Velours' 3
C. 'Ernest Markham' 2	C. 'Star of India' 2
C. 'Etoile Violette' 3	C. tangutica 3
C. 'Gipsy Queen' 3	C. 'The President' 2
C. 'Hagley Hybrid' 3	C. tibetana 3
C. 'H. F. Young' 2	C. 'Ville de Lyon' 3
	C. viticella 3
	C. 'Vyvyan Pennell' 2
	C. 'W. E. Gladstone' 2

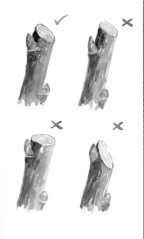

pruning cuts
Correct pruning cuts are very important to the health of all plants. Cuts should be sloping, just above a viable bud (above, top left).

wisteria

It is necessary to prune wisteria twice a year, once immediately after flowering and then again in the winter. Wisteria that is allowed to run free without any pruning soon runs out of flower-power. In late summer, cut back all the new growth to 6 in (15 cm) or four or five leaves. If you want to extend the plant's coverage, then leave a few shoots to grow on. In winter, reduce the stems even further to 3–4 in (7.5–10 cm) or two or three buds.

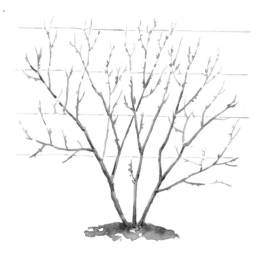

plants that flower on new wood
Plants that flower on fresh growth should be pruned in late winter or early spring.

late summer
Cut back all the new growth to 6 in (15 cm) or four or five leaves.

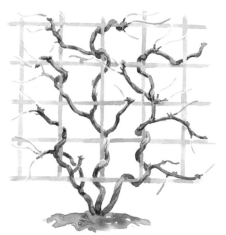

plants that flower on old wood
Plants that flower on the previous year's wood should be pruned directly after flowering. This will give them time to produce new shoots before winter.

winter
Cut back the stems even further than in the late summer, to 3–4 in (7.5–10 cm) or two or three buds.

other climbers

A simple pruning regime can make all the difference to the performance of a climber, but it is vital to know if the plant flowers on old or new wood. Follow these guidelines: remove all dead, diseased, and dying wood; cut out a few of the older stems to promote new, vigorous growth; do not allow plants to become tangled. Climbers that flower on old wood should be pruned immediately after flowering; those that flower on new wood should be left until late winter or spring.

ways of fixing plants to structures

A variety of devices and structures can be attached to walls and fences to give plants additional support. Wires can be discreet (see page 11 for attaching), wooden trellis decorative, and for smaller areas and plants that produce good leaf cover, rigid plastic mesh effective (although unattractive, which is why it needs to be hidden). For trellis, screw battens or blocks to the wall or fence (first drill holes into a wall with a masonry bit and use a plastic or wooden plug); these will make it easier to weave stems behind the trellis and to tie them in. Plastic mesh is attached using clips that can be either screwed or nailed in place. The mesh can be unclipped to allow pruning or maintenance of the supporting structure.

wires

Vine eyes are hammered or screwed into walls and the wire is fed through and secured at the ends.

trellis

Wooden battens or blocks should be attached to the boundary and the trellis secured to these.

plastic mesh with clips

The clips are attached to the boundary wall or fence and the mesh is held in place. The mesh can be unclipped for maintenance and access.

HEDGES

planting

Bare-rooted plants should be planted during the winter when the weather is neither too cold nor too wet. Container-grown plants can be planted at any time of the year as long as the weather is not too extreme and the plants are kept watered. Mulch to preserve moisture and to keep weeds down, and, if necessary, protect with a windbreak.

maintenance

Formal hedges need regular clipping to keep them neat and tidy, but even this, in the case of slow-growing plants such as yew and box,

only means once a year. More vigorous plants will need more frequent clipping. Use a template and string (see page 45) to ensure that the hedge is trimmed to a regular shape.

Informal hedges should be cut after flowering unless berries are required. They should be pruned rather than clipped, in the same way that you would prune a single shrub. There should be no attempt to cut them tight as you would with a formal hedge.

When clipping hedges, it can save a lot of time if you lay a large sheet on the ground to collect the trimmings. Do not leave clippings on the ground as grass and weeds will soon grow through them, making it difficult to remove both the clippings and the weeds. Shred and compost the pruned material and use it as a mulch and soil conditioner.

For good hedges, feed plants in the spring with a balanced slow-release fertilizer. There should be no need to water a hedge once it has become established.

TREES

Trees are frequently used along a boundary as a marker and to provide shelter and shade. Plant container-grown specimens at any time of year as long as the weather is not too extreme, but restrict the planting of bare-rooted trees to the winter months.

Before planting, dig a large hole and hammer a stake into it. Plant the tree, spreading out the roots around the stake. The depth of the tree should be the same as it was in the pot or in the nursery bed, as indicated by the soil mark on the stem. Backfill the hole with good soil and firm down. Use a tree-tie about 12 in (30 cm) above the soil to anchor the trunk to the stake. Keep watered until the tree has become established.

There is rarely a need to prune trees, other than fruit trees, except to remove dead or damaged branches, although it may be necessary to cut a tree back if it is getting too large or becoming misshapen.

staking trees

Anchor new trees with a tree-tie attached about 12 in (30 cm) from the ground.

WOODEN BOUNDARIES

Wood is a relatively cheap material for creating a boundary. It is very versatile, allowing for a wide range of shapes and styles, and generally not too difficult for the non-professional to use. Its life span is not as long as inert materials such as brick and stone but some timbers will last for many years, especially if regularly and thoroughly treated with preservative. Thin woods, particularly those covered with bark such as wattle hurdles, tend to last only a few years and should be considered as temporary fencing or screening.

choosing wood

Always choose the best quality wood you can afford. Hardwood lasts much longer than softwood but is very expensive. If possible, choose the wood yourself rather than simply ordering it. Look for seasoned wood, preferably free from knots and other defects. Select lengths that are not warped or deformed. "Sawn" (unplaned) timber is cheaper than "prepared" (planed) wood and will do for many fencing and trellis projects, but its surface is rough and therefore it is not suitable for painting and it may produce splinters. Prepared wood is smooth and is best for more refined structures and anything that needs a painted finish. Most lumberyards will cut and plane the wood to precisely the dimensions you require, which can save a lot of time and effort as well as provide a degree of accuracy that you may not be able to match.

preserving timber

It is possible to buy timber that has been treated with preservative. This is done under pressure, pushing the preservative much deeper into the grain of the wood than can be achieved by simply brushing it on. Treated wood is more expensive than untreated but the extra cost is worth it. All wooden structures should be treated every year with preservative. The best time to do this is during hot, dry weather when the wood is very porous and more likely to absorb the preservative. There are various preservatives available but avoid using the traditional creosote as this produces fumes that can have adverse effects on plants.

securing main posts

Whatever the quality of the wood and however well it has been preserved, if the structure is not secured properly, the fence or screen will be very short-lived, particularly if it is in an exposed position or is carrying the weight of climbers or other plants. The main posts of any permanent structure, and even temporary screens that must withstand wind and weight, must be concreted into the ground. As a rough guide, for every 12 in (30 cm) above the ground, allow foundations of 3 in (7.5 cm). So, for a 6-ft (1.8-m) fence, the main posts will need foundations of 18 in (45 cm). The hole should be larger than the post. Fill the bottom with broken rocks and secure the post with concrete. Again, rough proportions are one-third broken rocks to two-thirds concrete. For our example post, use 6 in (15 cm) of broken rocks and 12 in (30 cm) of concrete. Do not fill the hole to the top – cover with a layer of soil and turf.

main-post foundations
Always secure the main posts of wooden structures with concrete on a broken-rock base.

joining timber

The better the fit of joints, the less chance there is of water getting in and starting rot. However, the quality of joinery and trellising, especially in rustic structures, is rarely as high in fencing as it is in other forms of carpentry and so lack of experience should not be a deterrent. In many cases, a simple butt joint with long galvanized nails holding the two pieces of wood together is sufficient. Always use galvanized nails as ordinary steel nails rapidly corrode and work loose.

Properly made joints, however, are stronger and will last longer. These need not be the complicated dovetail joints of cabinetmaking; simple halved joints are among the most useful. Here, a section of wood, half the thickness of the piece of wood, is removed from each piece so that the two nestle together. The pieces of wood can be in a straight line, at right angles, or at a more oblique angle – the principle is the same in each case. Fix the joint with galvanized nails for most fencing but, for more sophisticated work, use glue and wooden dowels.

When hammering a nail into trelliswork or any structure that is not solid or is not lying flat on the ground, hold a heavy hammer on the opposite side of the wood to absorb the impact of the blow. This makes the job much easier.

butt joints

Butt joints are versatile, effective, and straightforward to make. Simply abut the two pieces of wood so that they sit neatly together, and secure with a long galvanized nail. The result is surprisingly solid.

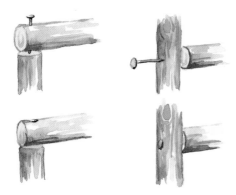

butt joints
The simplest joint, two pieces of wood are secured by a galvanized nail. No shaping is needed.

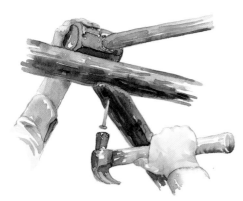

using a sledgehammer
When hammering a nail into a structure that is not on the ground, a hammer held on the opposite side of the wood will give stability.

birds-mouth joint
This simple joint comprises a niche removed from one piece of wood and a corresponding carved end in the other. Secure with galvanized nails.

halved joints

More complicated than butt joints, halved joints involve the removal of a section of wood from each of two pieces to be joined, cutting the same sized niche into half the thickness of each piece.

cutting a half-joint
Wedge the piece of wood so that it is firm, and slice out the joint using a chisel and hammer.

fitting a half-joint
Fit the two pieces together, adjusting as necessary, and secure them with a galvanized nail.

joints with dowels and glue

For a more professional finish, a wooden dowel should be used. Carve the joint and drill holes that will allow the dowel to fit tightly. Glue and secure with the dowel.

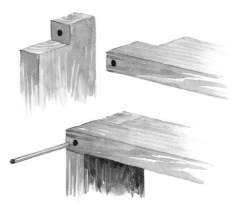

right-angle joints using a wooden dowel
A right-angle joint secured with a half joint, glue, and dowel is solid and neat in appearance.

cross-joints using a wooden dowel
A cross-shaped fixture can also be held together with glue and a dowel.

103

SOLID BOUNDARIES

For many, brick and stone walls are the ultimate in boundaries. Although the materials are expensive, walls can be long lasting and provide an ideal home for many climbing and tender plants. It is important that walls are well made, so if you have any doubts about your ability to build a secure, safe structure, employ a professional builder. However, two or three courses of bricks or walls up to 18 in (45 cm) in height should be within the ability of most gardeners.

foundations

All walls need foundations. On heavier soils, walls up to 2 ft (60 cm) in height need footings of 4 in (10 cm) of well-rammed broken rocks and 6 in (15 cm) of concrete. Walls above this need 4 in (10 cm) of broken rocks and 10 in (25 cm) of concrete. With softer ground the depth of concrete should be doubled. If in doubt, consult a builder. Foundations should be at least 2 in (5 cm) wider on each side than the width of the wall, and the top of the concrete should lie 2 in (5 cm) below the level of the ground to allow a recess for the first brick or stone. Foundations on sloping ground should be stepped and not run parallel to the ground.

basic foundations
Broken rocks and concrete should be used in well-calculated proportions for successful foundations.

foundations on a slope
Stepped foundations must be used on a slope to give a solid finish to a wall .

mixing concrete

Concrete can be bought ready to use, usually only in large quantities, but it is simple to make. Concrete is a mixture of cement, coarse sand, and aggregate, the last two usually being purchased ready mixed as "ballast." For foundations, a mixture of one part cement to five parts ballast is needed. The precise measurements are not critical, and it is usually made in shovelfuls, one of

cement to five of ballast. The easiest method is to use a mechanical concrete mixer. Add water a little at a time until the mixture is of the right consistency. Avoid making it too wet. To make concrete by hand, mix the dry ingredients on a large sheet of board. When thoroughly mixed, make a pile of the mixture and then open it up to form a crater. Pour water into the crater and stir the

hand-mixing concrete
1 *Mix the ingredients, pile them into the center of the board, and create a crater, with the mixture around the edge and a recess in the middle.*

2 *Slowly pour water into the crater; it should not run out of the recess.*

3 *Mix the concrete and the water, and add more water if necessary.*

cement and ballast into the center, mixing it with the water. Do not let the water escape. When all the water has been absorbed, mix thoroughly and add more water if necessary.

mortar
Mortar is made from a mixture of sand and cement powder. It is made in the same way as concrete in the proportions of four parts sand to one of cement. The mixture should have the consistency of soft butter. Adding a little liquid soap to the mix will make it more plastic and easier to use.

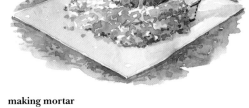

making mortar
Mortar needs the easy-spread consistency of soft butter. A little liquid soap can help.

brick walls
For most purposes, walls should be at least two bricks wide, that is 9 in (23 cm), although a single width of bricks can be used for walls of only two or three courses. The pattern that bricks make is important for strength as well as appearance. The common bonds are English bond and Flemish bond (both two-bricks thick) and running bond (a single-brick thickness).

Flemish bond
Two bricks deep, this bond has one, three, or five stretchers (bricks front-on) to one header (bricks side-on) per course.

running bond
A single brick deep, this bond comprises only stretchers (bricks front-on). These must be laid in a staggered formation for maximum strength.

English bond
Two bricks deep, this bond comprises whole courses of stretchers (bricks front-on), one, three, or five courses, to one course of headers (bricks side-on).

check level top and side
It is essential that walls are level in all directions, and a spirit level should be used constantly as the wall is built. Build the ends first and, using a line as a guide, build the center one row at a time.

raised beds

Raised beds can be a great asset in a garden, particularly where space is limited. They are very effective in small town gardens where they complement the adjacent house. Low structures, they are ideal for a novice builder. Raised beds of brick, stone, or concrete blocks need foundations. To provide drainage, leave gaps in the vertical pointing in the lower courses of the brickwork. A line of tiles toward the top will direct rainwater away from the brick surface. To prepare the bed, put a layer of broken rocks in the base and fill with good soil and organic material.

joining one wall to another

If joining a new wall to an existing one, the new wall can be keyed into the old one. Cut out bricks from every other course of the existing wall and insert bricks from the new wall. Alternatively, use wall ties that will firmly secure one wall into the other. Ties are available from building suppliers and come in many forms. Follow the instructions supplied. Both methods apply to straight walls and right-angles alike.

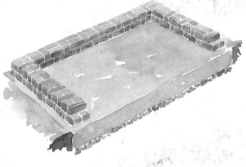

foundations
Create foundations of broken rocks and concrete, then build the raised bed, one course at a time. Larger beds need a two-brick-deep bond.

joining on a straight wall

Where an existing wall is being extended, neatly cut a brick out from every other course to form a toothed surface. Insert bricks from the new wall.

drainage
Drainage is provided by means of broken stones in the base and grit added to the soil and well-rotted organic material.

joining at right angles

1 *Carefully remove a runner from alternate course of bricks. These can be worked loose by chipping the mortar away.*

other materials
Railroad ties do not need foundations. Lay them on a flat base and stagger the vertical joins, leaving small gaps for drainage.

2 *Build the new wall into the niches, using the same bond as in the original wall and a spirit level to make sure the surfaces are straight.*

useful addresses

Plants, seeds, and bulbs

Blue Meadow Farm
184 Meadow Road
Montague
MA 01351

Bluestone Perennials
7211 Middle Ridge
Road
Madison
OH 44057

Burpee Seed Company
300 Park Avenue
Warminster
PA 18991-0001

Canyon Creek Nursery
3527 Dry Creek Road
Oroville
CA 95965

Carroll Gardens
P. O. Box 310
Westminster
MD 21158

Cultus Bay Nursery
4000 E. Bailey Road
Clinton
WA 98236

Dutch Gardens Inc.
P.O. Box 200
Department A58
Adelphia
NJ 07710

Jackson & Perkins
1 Rose Lane
Medford
OR 97501

Johnny's Selected
Seeds
305 Foss Hill Road
Albion
ME 04910

Mileager's Gardens
4838 Douglas Avenue
Racine
WI 53402

Montrose Nursery
P. O. Box 957
Hillsboro
NC 27278

Park Seed
Company, Inc.
1 Parkton Avenue
Greenwood
SC 29647

Rice Creek Gardens
1315 66 Avenue NE
Minneapolis
MN 55432

Shady Oaks Nursery
112 Tenth Avenue SE
Waseca
MN 56093

John Scheepers
23 Tulip Drive
Bantam
CT 06750

Smith Nursery Co.
P. O. Box 515
Charles City
IA 50616

Thomesville Nurseries
P. O. Box 7
Thomesville
GA 31792

Thompson & Morgan
P.O. Box 1308
Jackson
NJ 08527

Van Engelen Inc.
Stillbrook Farm
Maple Street, 307-B
Litchfield
CT 06759

André Viette Farm &
Nursery
Route 1, Box 16
Fishersville
VA 22939

Wayside Gardens
Highway 254
P. O. Box 1
Hodges
SC 29695-0001

We-Du Nurseries
Route 5, Box 724
Marion
NC 28752

White Flower Farm
30 Irene Street
Torrington
CT 06790

Woodlanders Inc.
1128 Colleton Avenue
Aiken
SC 29801

**Fencing, gates, and
trellis**

Bamboo Fences
179 Boylston Street
Boston
MA 02130

Colonial Garden
Products
P. O. Box 371008
El Paso
TX 79937

Joan Cook
P.O. Box 21628
Fort Lauderdale
FL 38335

French Wyres
P. O. Box 131655
Tyler
TX 75713

Gardener's Eden
P. O. Box 7307
San Francisco
CA 94120-9600

Gardener's Supply Co.
126 Intervale Road
Burlington
VT 05401

Smith and Hawken
2 Arbor Lane
P. O. Box 6900
Florence
KY 41022-6900

Treillage
420 S. 75th Street
New York City
NY 10021

**Lumber and building
supplies**

Home Depot
Check your local
telephone directory
for your nearest store

Lehigh Portland
Cement Co.
718 Hamilton Mall
Allentown
PA 18105

credits

The publishers would like to thank the following illustrators for their contribution to the book: Martine Collings, David Atkinson, Lizzie Saunders, Amanda Patton, and Anne Winterbotham. They would also like to thank the owners of the following gardens for their help:

Axletree Garden and Nursery, Peasmarch, East Sussex; Bates Green, Arlington, East Sussex; Beth Chatto Gardens, Elmstead Market, Essex; Cinque Cottage, Ticehurst, East Sussex; Grace Barrand Design Centre, Nutfield, Surrey; Hadspen Garden and Nursery, Castle Cary, Somerset; Hailsham Grange, Hailsham, East Sussex; Holkham Gardens, Wells-next-the-Sea, Norfolk; King John's Lodge, Etchingham, East Sussex; Marle Place, Brenchley, Kent; Sue Martin, Frittenden, Kent; Merriments Garden, Hurst Green, East Sussex; Queen Anne's, Goudhurst, Kent; Rogers Rough, Kilndown, Kent; Snape Cottage, Chaffeymoor, Dorset; Sticky Wicket Garden, Buckland Newton, Dorset; Upper Mill Cottage, Loose, Kent; Wyland Wood, Robertsbridge, East Sussex

All the photographs in this book were taken by Stephen Robson except for the following, which are courtesy of Jerry Harpur: p. 66; p.69; p. 92; p. 95.

index

F

Fagus sylvatica, 33, 34; *F. s.* 'Atropurpurea', 34
fences, 6, 48–49, 102; as animal-proofing, 37; curved, 52; picket, 49, 50–52; rustic, 52; temporary, 102
foundations; for a fence/screen, 102; picket fence, 51; and raised beds, 106; walls, 23, 104
fruit trees, 9, 18–20, 70, 101; frost protection, 20

G

gateways, 66–68; double, 48; internal, 66
Geranium dalmaticum, 24
grapes, 8, 18, 64
ground preparation, 96

H

hazel; hoops, 90; miniature hurdles, 89; rods, 70; wattle panels, 60
Hebe 'Midsummer Beauty', 38; *H. salicifolia*, 24, 38
hedges, 6, 30–31; archways in, 30; crenellated top, 34; feature, 40–42; formal, 32–34, 101; informal, 36–38, 101; low, 44–46; maintenance, 101; planting, 101; trimming, 33, 34, 45, 101
Helianthemum 'Rhodanthe Carneum', 24
Helianthus annuus 'Velvet Queen', 73
Helleborus foetidus, 46
holly, 30, 34
honeysuckle, 48, 64, 86
hornbeam, 34, 40, 41, 81
hurdles; edging, 70; miniature, 88–90; wattle *see* wattle panels

I

Ilex aquifolium, 30, 34
irises, 71
ivy, 98

J

jasmine, 48, 86
joints, 102–103; birds-mouth, 103; butt, 103; dovetail, 102; halved, 63, 102, 103; right-angle, 103

L

Lathyrus odoratus, 84
lavender, 49
lilac, 31
lime, 81
Linaria purpurea 'Canon Went', 15
Linum grandiflorum, 15
lumber; joining, 102; preserving, 103; "sawn" (unplaned), 102; lumberyards, 102
Lupinus 'Inverewe Red', 15
Lychnis flos-jovis, 24
Lythrum salicaria, 15

M

mirror, 92, 93
mulch, 36, 37, 97, 101; leaf, 97

N

nasturtiums, 48, 73
nectarines, 18

P

painting; picket fence, 51; picket gate, 68; *trompe l'oeil*, 92–94
panels, wattle, 48, 49, 58–60
passion fruit, 18
paths; function of, 6; and rose arches, 78; stepped, 70, 78
peaches, 18
pears, 18
peasticks, 84, 85
Penstemon 'Andenken an Friedrich Hahn', 15; *P. heterophyllus*, 16; *P.* 'Mother of Pearl', 24
perennials; as screening, 74; supporting, 15
pergolas, 54, 78
picket fences, 49, 50–52
picket gate, 66, 68
plant ties, 10, 11, 12, 14
plants; container-grown, 101; and creosote, 59, 64, 102; fixing to structures, 100–101; flowering on new wood, 100; flowering on old wood, 100; ground preparation, 96–97; *see also individual plants*
plaques, 8, 26
pleached trees, 6, 70, 71, 80–82
plums, 18
ponds, 26–28
posts; preparing, 51; securing, 51, 55, 102
pot marigolds, 74
preservative; for miniature hurdles, 90; for a picket fence, 51; for a rose arch, 78; for timber, 102; for a trellis, 56, 63, 64; for wattle panels, 59
pruning; clematis, 15, 56, 64, 99; climbing roses, 11, 12, 15, 98; cuts, 99; fruit trees, 19, 20, 101; hedges, 40, 41, 42, 45; pleached trees, 81, 82; roses, 37, 77, 98, 99; sweet peas, 85; wisteria, 100
pump, submersible, 26, 28

R

raised beds, 14, 106
Rosa 'Adélaïde d'Orléans', 76, 77; *R.* 'Iceberg', 46; *R.* 'Ispahan', 15, 24; *R.* 'Mme Alfred Carrière', 10, 11, 12; *R. rugosa*, 31, 36, 37; *R. r.* 'Alba', 37; *R.* 'White Pet', 24
roses; arches, 70, 76–78; hedges, 31; hips, 98; informal hedges, 37; rambling, 77, 98; trellis pillar, 70
rose, climbing, 9, 10, 11, 77, 98; maintaining, 12; planting, 11, 15; pruning, 11, 12, 15, 64,

98, 99; training, 11; trellis, 48, 64
runner beans, 70, 86

S

screens; formal hedges, 32; fruit trees, 70; function of, 6; internal, 60; plant, 72–74; protection from frost, 70; temporary, 84, 102; trellis, 49, 54; wattle panels, 60
shrubs, 10, 31, 36
sloping sites, 22, 23, 104
steps, 70, 78, 104
streams, 6, 70
sunflowers, 70, 72, 73
sweet chestnut, 88, 89

T

Taxus baccata, 30, 34; *T. b.* 'Aurea', 34
templates; gateway arches, 67; picket fence tops, 51; pruning, 45, 101; *trompe l'oeil* arch, 92
Thunbergia alata, 86
Tilia platyphyllos, 81
topiary, 31
trees; fruit, 9, 18–20, 70, 101; planting, 101; pleached, 6, 70, 71, 80–82; pruning, 101; staking, 101
trellis, 48, 49, 54–56, 100, 102; attaching, 100, 101; and climbers, 6, 48, 63; finials, 56; and gateway arch, 67; twining climbers, 98
Tropaeolum peregrinum, 86
tulips, 71

V

Verbascum bombyciferum, 24
Veronica 'Shirley Blue', 24
vine eyes, 10, 11, 12, 14, 101
violas, 44, 45, 46; *Viola cornuta*, 24; *V. riviniana*, 44, 46

W

walls, 6, 8–28, 104–106; brick, 104, 105; cascade, 26–28; fruit, 18–20; garden, 14–16; house, 10–11; joining at right angles, 106; joining one wall to another, 106; joining on a straight wall, 106; retaining, 22–24; stone, 104; tall, 23, 28
water features, 8, 26
weeds, 15, 96, 101
willow; cave, 41–42
windbreak netting, 32, 33
windbreaks, 32, 33, 59
wires, 100, 101; attaching, 11
wisteria, 100
wood, 102; choosing, 102; "prepared" (planed), 102; seasoned, 102; *see also* lumber
woodstain, 68, 94

Y

yew, 30, 31, 32, 34, 101

this

co   well as
he   lliant
de   rning

h